A GUIDE TO EVERYDAY ECONOMIC STATISTICS

Third Edition

Gary E. Clayton
Northern Kentucky University

Martin Gerhard Giesbrecht
Northern Kentucky University

McGRAW-HILL, INC.

New York   St. Louis   San Francisco   Auckland   Bogotá   Caracas   Lisbon
London   Madrid   Mexico City   Milan   Montreal   New Delhi
San Juan   Singapore   Sydney   Tokyo   Toronto

A GUIDE TO EVERYDAY ECONOMIC STATISTICS

1 2 3 4 5 6 7 8 9 0   DOC   DOC   9 0 9 8 7 6 5 4

ISBN 0-07-011336-X

The editor was Lucille Sutton;
the production supervisor was Elizabeth J. Strange.
R. R. Donnelley & Sons Company was printer and binder.

Dedication

It is traditional for authors to dedicate their work to their mentors, colleagues, and especially the family members and loved ones who have endured daily sacrifices while the authors dally at the keyboard. Well, we've done all of the above--and we certainly appreciate the support of our families and loved ones--but this time there is a special group we would like to acknowledge.

Specifically, we would like to dedicate this book to the many public servants in the Bureau of Economic Analysis, the Bureau of Labor Statistics, and the Bureau of the Census who are dedicated to making the statistics on the United States economy as good as they can possibly be.

We owe a special debt of thanks to numerous individuals--including Richard Bahr, Susan Behrmann, Sharon Cohany, Jeff Crawford, Pauline Cypert, Patrick Duck, Kevin Ellis, John Glaser, Patrick Jackman, Everette P. Johnson, Clint McCully, Jeff Newman, Nick Orsini, Kenneth Petrick, James Rankin, Steve Rawlings, Mary Lee Seifert, Chris Singleton, John Stinson, David Sullivan, Leeto Tlou, Brenda Yates, and Mary Young--who have answered questions, supplied data, recommended sources, and cheerfully tolerated a never-ending series of arcane (and sometimes inane) questions.

Finally, we are also indebted to Phil Yannarella, our government documents librarian, who can find *anything*. Of course, whatever errors and oversights remain in this manuscript are entirely our own, but we freely acknowledge that we could not have come this far without their help.

Indeed, in a world where government bureaucracy is becoming increasingly unpopular, we can report that there are some agencies that are a pleasure to work with. We'd like our readers to know that they are doing a great job. We'd like our colleagues in government to know that their efforts are sincerely appreciated.

About the Authors

Gary E. Clayton teaches economics and finance at Northern Kentucky University. He received his Ph.D. in Economics from the University of Utah, has taught economics and finance at several universities, and has authored a number of books and articles in educational, professional and technical journals. Dr. Clayton has appeared on a number of radio and television programs and, along with his colleague, Dr. Martin Giesbrecht, has appeared as a guest commentator for "Marketplace," which is broadcast on American Public Radio and originates at the University of Southern California.

Dr. Clayton also has a long-standing interest in economic education. He has participated in and directed numerous economic education workshops, received an Outstanding Citizen Certificate of Recognition from the state of Arkansas for his work in economic education, and was a national award winner in the college division of the International Paper Company competition which is sponsored by the National Council on Economic Education.

Martin Gerhard Giesbrecht teaches economics at Northern Kentucky University. He has taught and/or done research at Stanford University, the University of Chicago, Harvard University, Indiana University, National Chengchi University (Taiwan), Rutgers University, and Wilmington College. His doctoral degree (cum laude) was earned at the University of Munich, Germany, which he attended on a Fulbright Grant. Making economics accessible, intellectually enlightening, and even entertaining is the mission of Martin Giesbrecht's professional life. All of his ten books, including this one, and his many shorter articles, some of which have also appeared in German and Chinese, are dedicated to that end, as is his weekly commentary on WNKU.

Because he writes and speaks in a way that people can understand, the Society of Professional Journalism has bestowed its Award for Excellence on him in 1993. He has also won awards from the German-American Chamber of Commerce, the National Aeronautics and Space Administration (NASA), the American Society for Engineering Education, the National Science Foundation, The General Electric Foundation, the Ford Foundation, the U.S. Small Business Administration, and the National Endowment for the Humanities, among others.

Table of Contents

CHAPTER 5: SPENDING, SALES, AND EXPECTATIONS

CHAPTER 6: PRICES, MONEY, AND INTEREST RATES

CHAPTER 7: FINANCIAL MARKETS, INTERNATIONAL TRADE, AND FOREIGN EXCHANGE

APPENDIX: THE ECONOMIC BULLETIN BOARD

INDEX

Preface

Economic statistics, like so many other statistics, might seem as dry as an old bus schedule. A closer look, however, reveals them to be fascinating.

There are two reasons for this. One, economic statistics hit us where we can feel it: in the breadbasket, in our wallets, in our standards of living, and in our careers. And, two, they are themselves the product of one of the more extraordinary human endeavors of our modern age.

Statistics tell us a great deal about ourselves and our economy. Studying economics without paying attention to the statistics would be like a tourist ignoring a road map. But this book is neither a statistics lecture nor an economics textbook. Nor does it need to be read consecutively from beginning to end, although that is OK too. It is a handy little guide that can be consulted for clarification whenever any of the statistical series dealt with herein are encountered.

This book takes a closer look at the economic statistics that describe the world in which we live. It examines how the statistics are constructed and how we may use them effectively. Of course, we've had a lot of help along the way. This third edition has benefited not only from the suggestions of colleagues, students, and business decision makers, but also from the many members of the business news media, including the able staff of American Public Radio's *MARKETPLACE* program.

Use it well, and use it often.

Gary E. Clayton
Martin Gerhard Giesbrecht

Chapter 1

INTRODUCTION

How the Statistics in This Book Were Chosen

We need economic statistics to know how we are doing, and we need to know how we are doing in order to figure out how to get where we want to go. Decision making requires knowledge, and knowledge is the only logical basis of action. That is why we need economic statistics.

There are literally millions of statistical series! At the personal level, each of us could probably generate a dozen series from our grocery receipts, odometer readings, telephone bills, and electricity bills. Every business, town, city, county, and industry could do and often does the same in its own field of operation.

Even the broad-based measures of economic statistics, those that deal with whole states, regions, and nations, number into the thousands. A glance at any statistical yearbook or almanac or at the annual *Statistical Abstract of the United States*[1] will make this point.

Yet, only 35 series of economic statistics are dealt with in this book. Why?

First and most obvious, there is such a thing as too much information. It can prevent us from seeing the forest for all the trees.

---

[1] Available from the Superintendent of Documents, U.S. Government Printing Office, Washington, D.C. 20402, or any U.S. Department of Commerce district office.

Second, many statistical series, like one detailing our own personal electric consumption, are not interesting to everyone.

Third, many statistical series are compiled and published too late to be of much more than historical interest.

Finally, many statistical series are not reported regularly in the press and broadcast media. The 35 series dealt with in this book are those with extremely high profiles. Some, like the Dow Jones Industrial Average, are reported daily--on television, radio, and in national and local newspapers. Others, like the prime rate, are mentioned less frequently but receive prominent attention when they change.

If we want to know how we are doing or where we are headed, even just these 35 are usually more than enough. They include most of the major economic indicators that are important all of the time. Gross domestic product (GDP), the consumer price index, and the unemployment rate would certainly be in the top half-dozen of anyone's list of key economic statistics. Many others are important most of the time, and the rest are important at least some of the time.

We may not have selected everyone's favorite statistical series--and for that we apologize--but we are driven by a positive philosophy of wanting to describe "what is" rather than a normative one of "what should be." Many statistics are neglected when they should not be, while others are widely reported when there is less reason to do so. However, the objective here is to provide a guide to those series that *do* receive attention rather than to the ones that *should*.

A Frame of Reference

The main measure of overall economic and business activity is gross domestic product, whose fluctuations are the most important gauge of good times or bad times that we have. In this context, as in virtually all others, GDP is to be understood as a final, bottom-line accounting measure, an economic result, rather than as an indicator of things to come.

Many of the statistics reviewed in this book measure either the whole or parts of GDP. Other statistics, the index of 11 leading indicators preeminent among them, serve better as signals of things to come. There are also the more specialized series, such as new housing starts and Standard & Poor's 500 (S&P 500), that serve both as general indicators of future economic activity and as first-order indicators for their own industries. Finally, we have other series such as domestic auto sales that provide important information for their respective industries but have almost no value as indicators of future economic activity.

As we peruse the formal world of economic statistics, bear in mind that they cannot be evaluated in a vacuum. Statistical series need a background, or a frame of reference, so that they can be put in proper perspective. This the book attempts to do. Sometimes the frame of reference is discussed in terms of the historical development and evolution of the series. Or, the perspective may take the form of a detailed discussion of the way the statistic is measured and compiled. The frame of reference may also be the way the particular indicator or statistic relates to other developments in the economy. In the end, our goal is to provide a perspective that allows for proper interpretation and application of the particular series.

Of particular interest in Figure 1-1 are the three types of indicators: leading, lagging, and coincident. The name given to each refers to the way the series moves in relation to changes in overall economic activity. For example, the series marked "leading indicator" turns down before the economy enters a recession (the shaded area in the figure) and turns up before the expansion begins.

The "lagging indicator" series behaves just the opposite: it turns down after the economy enters a recession, and up sometime after the recovery is underway. A coincident indicator neither leads nor lags. Instead, its timing is such that it turns down when the economy turns down, and up when the economy turns up.

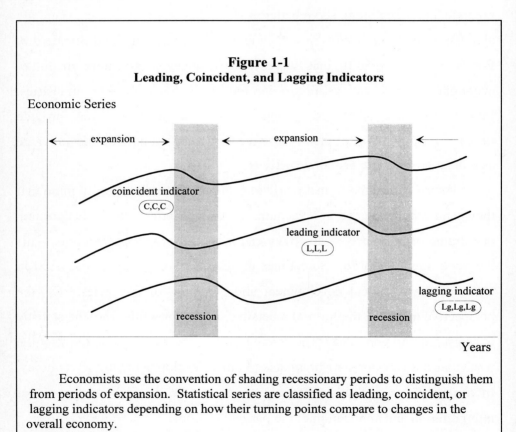

Figure 1-1
Leading, Coincident, and Lagging Indicators

Economic Series

expansion ⟶   ⟵ expansion ⟶   ⟵

coincident indicator
(C,C,C)

leading indicator
(L,L,L)

lagging indicator
(Lg,Lg,Lg)

recession   recession

Years

Economists use the convention of shading recessionary periods to distinguish them from periods of expansion. Statistical series are classified as leading, coincident, or lagging indicators depending on how their turning points compare to changes in the overall economy.

The three codes in the oval key for each indicator show how the changes in the individual series compare to changes in the overall economy. The coding, also shown in Figure 1-2, is the same as that used by the Bureau of Economic Analysis (BEA) in the Department of Commerce to classify the economic indicators reported in the monthly *Survey of Current Business*.

Sometimes a series leads both peaks and troughs in the economy to make it an overall leading indicator. At other times, it may lead peaks and lag troughs to earn an overall rating of "unclassified." Other series play no role as indicators of overall economic activity, and so no codes are shown.

Figure 1-2
Leading, Lagging, and Coincident Indicators

(L,Lg,U)   The series leads the peaks in the economy; it turns down *before* the economy turns down (L = leads).
The series lags the economic recovery; it turns up *after* the economy turns up (Lg = lags).
Overall, the series is unclassified; it is neither a leading nor a lagging indicator on a consistent basis (U = unclassified).

(Lg,C,Lg)   The series turns down *after* the economy peaks (Lg = lags).
The series recovers *just as* the economy recovers (C = coincident).
Overall, the series lags (Lg = lags) as an economic indicator.

(C,L,L)   The series turns down *just as* the economy turns down (C = coincident).
The series turns up *before* the economy turns up (L = leads).
Overall, the series is classified as a leading indicator (L = leads) even though the timing of the series is coincident for peaks.

The first code in the oval stands for the timing of the series with respect to peaks in the economy, or when the expansion ends and the recession begins. The second stands for the timing of the series with respect to troughs in the economy, or when the recession ends and the recovery begins. The last code indicates the overall classification of the indicator.

Whenever possible, the economic series examined in this book are plotted against the historical background of recessions and expansions. As will be seen, many series behave like those in Figure 1-1, although the timing of the turning points will vary considerably. Others will appear to have little, if any, relationship to changes in the overall economy. Even so, we feel that the presentation is important if you are to make your own judgments about the behavior of the series.

We have also listed convenient sources of data. Sometimes the source is in the form of easily accessible publications, and sometimes it is in the form of a telephone hotline. There is also an appendix at the end of this book describing an electronic bulletin board available at the U.S. Department of Commerce to anyone with a personal computer and modem. Each of these sources will help you keep abreast of your own favorite series.

The Many Faces of Economic Statistics

The task of interpretation might seem to be a simple one: just take the numbers and describe how they have changed. Unfortunately, it's not always that easy. The task of interpretation is also made difficult because most statistical series can be reported in a number of ways. To illustrate, consider a hypothetical report stating that total sales increased from $900 billion to $940 billion over a recent 12-month period. If the report is in terms of current prices, and many initial reports are released this way, then it stands to reason that some of the $40 billion increase is due to inflation.

To compensate for inflation, sales can be measured in terms of constant dollars--also known as real dollars--using prices that prevailed in an earlier year. If 1987 is used as the base year, then the same report could be worded like this: "In terms of constant 1987 dollars, total sales increased from $630 billion to $643 billion for the most recent year." Since prices were about 30 percent lower in 1987 than they are today, the $900 billion is converted to $630 billion for purposes of the report.

Most series that are susceptible to the distortions of inflation are reported in both current (nominal) and constant (real) dollar amounts, with

1987 being the most popular base year. Both kinds of information are valuable--if used correctly--although the availability of both means that final sales statistics can be reported in a number of different ways:

- the *current* or *nominal* dollar value of total sales ($940 billion)
- the change in the *current* or *nominal* dollar value of total sales ($40 billion)
- the *constant*, or *real* dollar value, of total sales ($643 billion)
- the change in the *constant*, or *real* dollar value, of total sales ($13 billion)
- the percentage change in the *current* or *nominal* dollar sales (4.44 percent, or $40 billion/$900 billion)
- the percentage change in the *constant* or *real* dollar sales (2.06 percent, or $13 billion/$630 billion)[2]

We have the same type of problem when numbers are converted to an index, such as the consumer price index, the producer price index, or any other index. For example, suppose that the index under consideration has a base year of 1977 = 100 and currently stands at 145. If the index goes to 146 in the next month, there is an increase of 1 over the base period activity, or a 0.69 percent increase in the index over the previous month (1/145 = 0.0069). If the index were to grow at the same rate for each of the next 11 months, the annualized rate would be 8.6 percent.[3]

Using the numbers in the paragraph above, we can see that the change in any index can be reported in several different ways:

- the *absolute level* of the index (145)
- the *absolute change* in the level or the index from period to period (1)
- the *relative percentage change* from the previous period (0.69 percent)
- an *annualized projection* of the current period percentage change (8.6 percent)

---

[2] If the nominal change was 4.44 percent, and if the real, or price-adjusted change was 2.06 percent, then the 2.38 percent difference was due to inflation.
[3] The series is compounding monthly, and so the correct computation is to use the following formula:

$$\text{Annualized growth} = (1 + \text{monthly percentage change})^{12} - 1$$
$$= (1 + 0.0069)^{12} - 1 = 0.086$$

Because of compounding, you *cannot* multiply the monthly percentage change of 0.0069 by 12 to get an annualized rate, although some people often make this mistake!

In general, the relative percentage change is the most useful, with the annualized version coming in next. However, the reader should be advised that even these lists are not exclusive. For example, sometimes the change in the level of the index is compared to a period 12 months earlier. If the new level of 146 is 10 points higher than it was 12 months ago, then we could also say that the annual increase was closer to 7.35 percent.

Abusing Economic Statistics

The governments of the modern, industrialized nations of the free world--the United States among the best of them--enjoy a remarkable reputation for producing honest statistics. Surprisingly (since they bear less responsibility to the citizenry), so do many nongovernmental agencies in these countries that produce statistical series, some of which are included in this book. In some nations however, statistics are exaggerated, underreported, or simply faked for political or ideological reasons. When this happens, the usefulness of the statistics is radically reduced. Whether they know it or not, it is also a tragic loss to those nations that support this type of activity.

In the United States, it has been hinted that the release of new statistical figures is sometimes delayed for a few hours in order to prevent some political or commercial embarrassment. But even such temporary mischief has not been widely confirmed. Quite to the contrary, what no politician or business leader in America will deny is that statistics tend to be brutally honest.

Perhaps the most common abuse of economic statistics is to apply them to situations for which they were never intended. For example, some series with little, if any, relationship to movements of the overall economy are often treated as if they are significant predictors of future changes in GDP. Personal income in current dollars, discussed in detail in Chapter 4, is one such example. The historical record shows that personal income almost always goes up, even when the economy is in recession.[4] Even so, increases in personal income are dutifully reported and widely heralded by the press each time they are released.

Other series are treated as indicators of future overall economic activity when in fact they consistently lag developments in the economy. Interest rates can be cited in this context. For the most part, interest rates tend to follow, rather than lead, changes in the overall economy. Declining interest rates may benefit some sectors of the economy, especially housing, automobiles, and to some extent stock prices, but lower interest rates are of little use in predicting future changes in the overall economy.

Yet a third abuse is to focus on nominal dollar values when the real, or inflation-adjusted, figures give a better picture of the underlying changes. Unfortunately, the various government agencies contribute to this problem because the nominal dollar data and the price deflators needed to adjust the data are not available at the same time. When the U.S. Department of Commerce releases its *Advance Monthly Retail Sales* report[5] during the second week of every month, the data are adjusted for seasonal, holiday, and trading day differences but not for inflation. By the time inflation-adjusted figures are available, the initial change in retail sales has already been reported and the new figures are of little interest to the media.

Finally, we should note that the media sometimes report on new government figures without giving us enough information to evaluate the

---

[4] The most recent recession in the U.S. economy began in July 1990. During the 9 recessionary months that followed, personal income in current dollars increased 7 times and declined only twice! In terms of constant dollars, there were 5 monthly decreases and 4 increases.

[5] A brief monthly report available on a subscription basis from the Superintendent of Documents, U.S. Government Printing Office, Washington, DC 20402.

significance of the numbers. It is not at all unusual to hear that a particular index has gone up, say, 4 points, without any mention of the overall level of the index. Four points on a basis of 40 is one thing, but 4 points on an index with a value of 400 may be quite another.

Using Economic Statistics

Decision making often requires an understanding of regional or industry-specific economic conditions. Even if the data you need are not described in these chapters (most of the statistics in this book pertain to the national economy), you should be able to use the methodology described here to make your own decisions or even build your own set of economic indicators.

If you do, remember that every statistical series has its own distinct personality. If you want to use a series, study it carefully and try to see how it relates to your own situation. For example, are series measured in real, rather than nominal, dollars better for your application? Also, you might examine the series to see if changes in the series are more important than the absolute level of the series. And what about the timing of the series? If it lags, then it may not be of much help. If it leads, then you may have to spend more time trying to anticipate its movements. If you need regional or industry-specific data, don't forget to look for other sources of data generated by state departments of economic development, chambers of commerce, economic development districts, local universities, and industry and trade publications.

One practical way of organizing economic statistics for your own use is to build your own historical data base of the statistical series that are especially important to you. You can do this with an appropriate spreadsheet program on your personal computer, or you can do it just as well on paper marked off with rows for years and columns for the individual statistical series (or vice versa). Yearly entries are probably sufficient for the bygone years; quarterly and monthly data for more recent times will keep you more up-to-date.

To monitor overall economic conditions, you may want to keep tabs on GDP, the consumer price index, the unemployment rate, and several other series, such as the index of leading indicators. To zero in on your own individual area of concern, focus on those series that affect this area more directly. For example, you would examine consumer spending and retail sales if your concern is retail marketing, or the Dow Jones Industrial Average and Standard & Poor's 500 if you're more concerned with the stock market.

As your sophistication grows, this accumulation of statistical data will not only reveal the current state of affairs to you, but you will begin to be able to discern the development of trends. Being able to do this on your own this way, rather than relying on the news media that everybody reads, hears, and watches, gives you that decisive competitive edge that is so important in today's business. It's mighty useful in your personal affairs too.

Finally, be creative. If the statistics enable you to perceive your economic reality, your economic reality may also enable you to anticipate the statistics. This can be very useful. For example, if your decision is to refinance a mortgage and if you are waiting for the lowest possible rates, it helps to know that interest rates usually lag changes in the national economy. If the economy is currently in recession, you can usually expect mortgage rates to go down and continue to go down during the early part of the expansion. In this case, it might be wise to postpone the refinancing for several months. Or, if the expansion is well underway, you may want to refinance immediately since interest rates have a history of increasing late in the recovery and even during the early part of the recession. In either case, knowledge of how a series relates to the overall economy can be helpful when it comes to forecasting changes in the series.

And Beware of Forecasts!

None of this is a formal theory and method for making forecasts. Much longer books than this have dealt unsuccessfully with that subject. But we do encounter many large and small forecasts in our daily lives, and these contain fertile opportunities for making statistical trouble. Be forewarned! Here are some things to look out for:

Point Forecasts These are the most common, but they are often wrong because outcomes are unlikely to reach the predicted point precisely. For example, if we predict that the GDP next year will be $8 trillion, we have an almost 100 percent chance of being wrong because next year's GDP might turn up to $8 trillion and 1 cent or any other such number.

Interval Forecasts It is better to say that next year's GDP will be $8 trillion, give or take $50 billion. That means the forecast will turn out to be correct if next year's GDP falls between $7.95 and $8.05 trillion.

Probability Forecasts It is even better to say that next year's GDP has an 85 percent probability of being between $7.95 trillion and $8.05 trillion. This way the confidence with which the forecast is made can be expressed. The higher the probability, the more believable the forecast should be, assuming that the forecaster is reputable.

Unconditional Forecasts All of the above examples fall into this category because, unlike the conditional forecast below, they are not premised on some second event taking place.

Conditional Forecasts "There is an 85 percent probability that next year's GDP will be between $7.95 trillion and $8.05 trillion if the Federal Reserve System does not raise the discount rate" is a conditional forecast. If the Fed does, in fact, raise the discount rate, all bets are off.

Event Forecasts All the above examples fall into this category because they deal with a single event, a single outcome.

Time Series Forecasts A series of forecasts that march into the future by convenient time steps--weeks, months, quarters, or years--are much more complicated than a single-event forecast. For example, forecasting that "the GDP next year will grow at an annual rate of 4 percent during the first 6 months and then slow to 3 percent in the last half of the year" is actually making at least two forecasts. Since the second one is probably dependent on the accurate outcome of the first, this kind of forecasting can be tricky. Rate-of-change-over-time forecasts are especially susceptible to this complication.

Extrapolation Forecasts Extrapolation from a monthly figure is almost a special time series forecast. For example, a monthly increase of 0.69 percent converts to an annual rate of 8.6 percent if the next 11 months are identical to the most recent one.

Weighted Moving Average Forecasts If a particular series is subject to considerable fluctuation, a moving average with specific weights assigned to earlier periods can be used to smooth the data[6] When this technique is adapted to forecasting, it is easier to predict the next number in the average since a portion of the data used to construct it is already in hand. And, with our attention focused on the moving average, the forecaster can even be excused if the next new observation "deviates" from the mean.

Many of the forecasts that we encounter in the daily news have considerable value. Many others, however, have little or no value since we are not clear as to what kind of forecast they are or how they have been constructed. They often use hedging or waffling language that, when carefully read or listened to, pulls the rug of credibility out from underneath them. Even worse, many are based on other statistics that may not be well-suited for the forecast being made.

A Final Word

Throughout, this book intends to be ideologically and theoretically neutral or at least conventional. Notice that the economic indicators described in the following chapters are grouped primarily by economic function rather than by alphabet or other method. This is to recognize implicitly that while no formal theoretical or ideological statement is

---

[6] Statistics on changes in manufacturing and trade inventories are smoothed using a four-term weighted average with weights of 1, 2, 2, 1. To illustrate, changes of $-47.2, $68.2, $64.1, and $40.3 billion (the numbers for June, July, August, and September of 1990) yield a moving average of $42.95 billion for the month of September.

intended, our economy is nevertheless a functioning system made up of identifiable parts that somehow work together.

And remember: we should never become so blinded by the apparent numerical precision and by the "scientific," "theoretical," or "official" nature of these economic indicators that we ignore our own sensitivity to economic and business conditions. Our own observations may be rather parochial, but they are immediate and undisputably real. Keeping an eye on the amount of construction activity in the neighborhood where we live, the intensity of traffic on our streets, how hard or easy it is to find a place to park, what and how much people are buying in the stores where we shop, the number of layoffs or job promotions among our friends and acquaintances, the level of maintenance and upkeep in our surrounding buildings and grounds, and even the changes in the frequency of marriages and new babies in our communities can all be very revealing. We ourselves are, after all, living daily in the very economy we are trying to understand.

This economic awareness, this "feel" for business conditions should be extended to our interpretations of the statistical series as well. We can examine the way statistical series are constructed, and we can look at the historical record to see how they behave. But in the end, it comes down to developing a feel for what they really tell us.

Chapter 2

TOTAL OUTPUT, PRODUCTION, AND GROWTH

Gross Domestic Product

The most comprehensive measure of production is **gross domestic product** (**GDP**)--the market value of all final goods, services, and structures produced in 1 year by labor and property located in the United States, regardless of who owns the resources. In 1991, the Bureau of Economic Analysis switched to GDP from GNP (where N stands for national), which is a measure of the total income produced in 1 year with labor and property supplied by U.S. residents, regardless of where the resources are located.[1]

How Is GDP Measured?

Because GDP is such a comprehensive measure, it is not practical to record every final good, service, or structure produced in the course of one year. Instead, sampling techniques are used and projections are made from the samples.

It helps to think of the analysis as being divided into two parts. The first involves a count of the number of final goods, services, and structures

---

[1] The conversion to GDP makes the measurement of total output consistent with the system of accounts used by the World Bank and most other industrial nations--including Japan, Canada, and the United Kingdom. The difference between GNP and GDP (explained in detail in Chapter 4) is relatively small, ranging from -1.4 percent to +0.05 percent from 1947 until the first quarter of 1994.

produced. The second involves assigning a dollar value to the output. If current or nominal market prices are used, then the measure is simply *GDP*, or *GDP in current prices*. If we want to adjust for the distortions of inflation, we value the output using base year prices to get *real GDP*, or *GDP in constant prices*.

Table 2-1 illustrates both types of computations for the U.S. economy in the first quarter of 1994. Suppose that the items in the first column represent actual production in that year. If output is valued at the prices that existed at the time, the total value of production--or GDP in current dollars-- amounted to $6,623.1 billion. In the bottom part of the table, the same output is valued at the prices that prevailed in 1987, the base year currently used by

Table 2-1
Computation of GDP in Millions of Current and Constant Dollars

(A) GDP in Current Prices:

Annual Domestic Output		Quantity in millions	1994 Prices	Value in millions of $
Goods:	Automobiles	7	$19,500	$136,500
	Chairs	5	80	400
	.....Other	--	--	--
Services:	Legal	8	550	4,400
	Child care/wk	3	80	240
	.....Other	--	--	--
Structures:	Residential	1.4	140,000	196,000
	Commercial	1	340,000	340,000
	.....Other	--	--	--
	GDP in Current Dollars			*$6,623,100*

(B) GDP in Constant (1987) Prices:

Annual Domestic Output		Quantity in millions	1987 Prices	Value in millions of $
Goods:	Automobiles	7	$16,219	$113,533
	Chairs	5	65	325
	.....Other	--	--	--
Services:	Legal	8	412	3,296
	Child care/wk	3	60	180
	.....Other	--	--	--
Structures:	Residential	1.4	114,740	160,636
	Commercial	1	269,469	269,469
	.....Other	--	--	--
	GDP in Constant (1987) Dollars			*$5,269,500*

the U.S. Department of Commerce.[2] This measure gives us GDP in constant (1987) dollars of $5,269.5 billion.

The advantage of using constant prices is that it enables us to compare the annual rate of total output in the first quarter of 1994 to the third quarter of 1993, or to any other year and quarter, for that matter. So if real GDP in 1994 changes by 1 or 2 percent, the difference *must* be due to changes in the number of goods, services, and/or structures produced. The increase *cannot* be due to inflation since prices were held constant.[3]

GDP Estimates and Revisions

GDP estimates are made quarterly, and additional revisions are made as new data become available. The Bureau of Economic Analysis (BEA) in the U.S. Department of Commerce releases three estimates according to the following schedule:

Advance--released near the end of the *first* month after the end of the quarter.

Preliminary--released near the end of the *second* month after the end of the quarter.

Final--released near the end of the *third* month after the end of the quarter.

Figure 2-1 shows the above three estimates from the third quarter of 1992 through the first quarter of 1994. As you can see, the three estimates for any one quarter are usually fairly close, but they can be off by as much as 1½ percentage points or more.

---

[2] The 1991 comprehensive revision of the national income and product accounts (NIPA) established 1987 as the base year for constant dollar prices. To convert a $6,623.1 billion current GDP to 1987 dollars, we divide the current measure by the implicit GDP price deflator--a type of inflation index for GDP--and then multiply by 100. Or, ($6,623.1/125.7)100 = $5,269.5 if we ignore a minor error due to rounding. Finally, because the prices of some products increase faster than others, separate price deflators are used for each (110.4 was the price deflator used for durable goods, 135.8 for services, and 120.3 for structures).

[3] Whenever a series is converted to constant dollars or prices, only the *percentage change* is relevant, not the constant dollar value of the series. As long as we focus on percentage changes, the choice of the base year is not important. Most series measured in dollars have converted to a 1987 base year, although other series often use other years: the *index of help-wanted advertising* uses 1967 for a base year; *Standard & Poor's 500* uses 1941-1943 as the base period, and the *index of consumer expectations* uses the first quarter of 1966 as its base period.

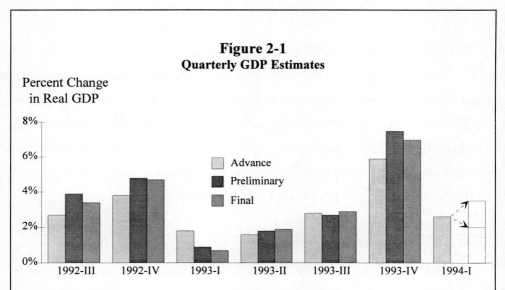

Figure 2-1
Quarterly GDP Estimates

The monthly revisions of quarterly GDP can vary substantially from one month to the next. Between 1979 and 1990, two-thirds of the final revisions were within -0.6 to +0.9 percent of the advance estimate. On this basis, in April the Bureau of Economic Analysis estimated that the final 1994 first-quarter change in real GDP would likely fall between 2.0 and 3.5 percent.[4] In June 1994, the final GDP estimate was revised to 3.4 percent.

Because of the revisions and delays in getting the estimates, we really don't know how the economy fared during a particular quarter until nearly 3 months later--and even these estimates are reviewed annually every July for the most recent calendar year and the two preceding years. For example, in July 1995, the final GDP figures for 1994, 1993, and 1992 will all be revised.

Last but not least, even more comprehensive revisions are carried out at approximately 5-year intervals. This means that we never have the luxury of just adding the latest numbers to a time series such as that shown in Figure 2-2. Instead, we always have to obtain the most recent historical revisions if we want to look at the long-term trends.[5]

---

[4] Nine-tenths of the revisions fell between -1.1 and +1.6 percent or the advance estimate. Source: File GDP.BEA released April 28, 1994, on THE ECONOMIC BULLETIN BOARD. This file is updated monthly as new estimates become available.

[5] Some monthly numbers, like the *purchasing manager's index* described on pages 34-37, are never revised subsequent to their initial release.

Does GDP Overlook Anything?

You bet! For example, GDP tells us nothing about the *mix,* or *composition* of output. A bigger GDP only tells us that the dollar value of total output increased. We don't know if the increase was due to the production of new homes, schools, and libraries--or, to the increased production of nerve gas, B-1 bombers, and toxic waste landfills. Also, GDP doesn't tell us anything about the *quality of life.* For example, you might feel that the quality of life is enhanced every time a city park or museum is built instead of a nuclear reactor.

Perhaps the biggest limitation is that GDP excludes nonmarket activities, such as the services performed by homemakers and the services people perform for themselves. For example, GDP will go down if a homeowner marries his or her housekeeper and does not hire a replacement. Likewise, GDP will go up if you hire someone to mow your own yard, but it will not go up if you do it yourself.

Other activities--prostitution, gambling, and drug running--are mostly illegal and are simply not reported to the IRS, Department of Commerce, or anyone else. These activities are part of the underground economy and are not directly included in GDP, although estimates are made for their inclusion.[6]

When Is the Economy in a Recession?

A recession occurs whenever real GDP declines for two consecutive quarters. However, the exact date a recession begins and ends is not determined by the Bureau of Economic Analysis or any other government

---

[6] In December 1985, GNP statistics extending back to 1929 were revised upward to account for the unreported activity in the underground economy. As a result of the revision, GNP in 1984 was increased by $119.9 billion (these revisions are now part of GDP). As large as this may seem, many economists in the private sector felt that the revisions were not large enough!

Table 2-2
Business Cycle Expansions and Contractions in the United States

| Peak | Trough | Peak | Duration in Months* | | |
			Recession	Expansion	Cycle
	December 1854	June 1857	--	30	--
June 1857	December 1858	October 1860	18	22	40
October 1860	June 1861	April 1865	8	*46*	*54*
April 1865	December 1867	June 1869	*32*	18	*50*
June 1869	December 1870	October 1873	18	34	52
October 1873	March 1879	March 1882	65	36	101
March 1882	May 1885	March 1887	38	22	60
March 1887	April 1888	July 1890	13	27	40
July 1890	May 1891	January 1893	10	20	30
January 1893	June 1894	December 1895	17	18	35
December 1895	June 1897	June 1899	18	24	42
June 1899	December 1900	September 1902	18	21	39
September 1902	August 1904	May 1907	23	33	56
May 1907	June 1908	January 1910	13	19	32
January 1910	January 1912	January 1913	24	12	36
January 1913	December 1914	August 1918	23	*44*	*67*
August 1918	March 1919	January 1920	*7*	10	*17*
January 1920	July 1921	May 1923	18	22	40
May 1923	July 1924	October 1926	14	27	41
October 1926	November 1927	August 1929	13	21	34
August 1929	March 1933	May 1937	43	50	93
May 1937	June 1938	February 1945	13	*80*	*93*
February 1945	October 1945	November 1948	*8*	37	*45*
November 1948	October 1949	July 1953	11	*45*	*56*
July 1953	May 1954	August 1957	*10*	39	*49*
August 1957	April 1958	April 1960	8	24	32
April 1960	February 1961	December 1969	10	*106*	*116*
December 1969	November 1970	November 1973	*11*	36	*47*
November 1973	March 1975	January 1980	16	58	74
January 1980	July 1980	July 1981	6	12	18
July 1981	November 1982	July 1990	16	92	108
July 1990	March 1991		8	--	--

Averages for peacetime cycles (recession and expansion) only:*

	1854-1991 (26 cycles)		19	27	48
	1854-1919 (14 cycles)		22	24	47
	1919-1945 (5 cycles)		20	26	45
	1945-1991 (7 cycles)		11	43	54

*Cycles are measured from peak to peak; a trough to trough measurement gives different durations. The underscored figures are wartime periods.
Source: National Bureau of Economic Research and the *Survey of Current Business.*

agency. Instead, the turning points are determined by the National Bureau of Economic Research (NBER), a prestigious private research institute with a long and distinguished record of research into the cause and measurement of business cycles.

Because the NBER wants to determine the turning points as accurately as possible, it considers as much data as it can, most of it monthly. As a result, the official turning points, listed in Table 2-2 and illustrated in Figure 2-2, may not always coincide with quarterly changes in real GDP.

According to the NBER, the record expansion of the 1980s ended in July 1990, which coincided with the third-quarter decline in real GDP. However, the determination of the July turning point was not made until much later in May 1991 after members of the NBER business cycle dating committee examined historical data on jobs, personal income, industrial production, and retail, manufacturing, and trade sales. Likewise, the official ending date of March 1991 was not announced until December 1992--nearly

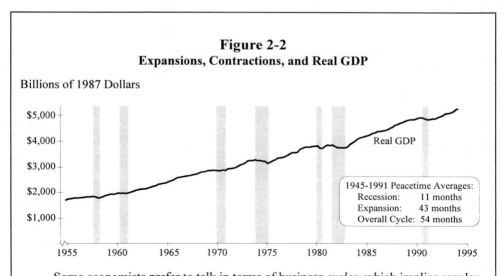

Figure 2-2
Expansions, Contractions, and Real GDP

Billions of 1987 Dollars

1945-1991 Peacetime Averages:
Recession: 11 months
Expansion: 43 months
Overall Cycle: 54 months

Some economists prefer to talk in terms of business *cycles*, which implies regular and systematic changes in real GDP marked by alternating periods of expansion and contraction. Others prefer to talk in terms of business *fluctuations*, which implies alternating periods of expansion and contraction but on a less than systematic basis.

21 months later.[7]

How Are Other Statistics Related to GDP?

Good question! In fact, most of the statistics reported in this book are related to GDP in one way or another. Some statistics report on the various components of total output--goods, services, structures, exports, and so on. Other statistics are used more as indicators to help predict future changes in the level of GDP.

Table 2-3
The National Income and Product Accounts,
First Quarter 1994--Billions of Current and Constant 1987 Dollars

	Current	Constant	% GDP
Gross domestic product	***$6,623.1***	***$5,269.5***	***100.0***
Personal consumption expenditures	***4,563.7***	***3,551.9***	***68.9***
Durable goods	578.0	523.4	8.7
Nondurable goods	1,382.5	1,111.8	20.9
Services	2,603.2	1,916.6	39.3
Gross private domestic investment	***970.0***	***889.3***	***14.6***
Fixed investment	949.1	868.7	14.3
Nonresidential	668.4	636.8	10.1
Structures	178.2	148.2	2.7
Producers' durable equipment	490.2	488.6	7.4
Residential	279.1	232.2	4.2
Change in business inventories	20.9	20.6	0.3
Net exports of goods and services	***-83.5***	***-105.0***	***-1.3***
Exports	678.2	615.6	10.2
Imports	761.7	720.6	11.5
Government purchases of goods and services	***1,172.9***	***933.3***	***17.7***
Federal	440.9	344.3	6.7
National defense	291.7	227.5	4.4
Nondefense	149.3	116.7	2.3
State and local	732.0	589.0	11.1

Source: File GDP.BEA, June 29, 1994, THE ECONOMIC BULLETIN BOARD. The numbers shown in the table are the final GDP revision for the first quarter of 1994. The appendix at the end of this book discusses this source in more detail. Some totals may not agree because of rounding. Percent of GDP column based on current dollars; percentages are slightly different for constant dollars.

---

[7] The members of the committee included seven prominent economists: Robert E. Hall of the Hoover Institute at Stanford University (chairman of the dating committee), Geoffry Moore of Columbia University, Robert J. Gordon of Northwestern University, Benjamin M. Friedman of Harvard University, Victor Zarnowitz of the University of Chicago, William Branson of Princeton University, and Martin Feldstein of Harvard University (also president of the NBER).

In either case, it may help to examine Table 2-3 which shows one view of GDP as it appears in the national income and product accounts (NIPA), the system of accounts used to track the nation's production, consumption, and income statistics. In the view shown in Table 2-3, GDP is broken down according to its consumption by sector--consumer, business or investment, export, and government.

Some statistics measure the overall performance of a major heading such as personal consumption expenditures. Other series track subcategories like durable and nondurable goods.[8] Even others are used to track the production of individual products like automobiles and residential housing.

The production of GDP also generates wages and salaries for individuals and profits for business owners. Since these groups eventually spend their income, more statistics are kept on the income and/or spending of these groups. Almost every statistic, then, is related to GDP in one way or another. As we shall see, it is always useful to keep the relationship between an individual statistic and overall GDP in mind when evaluating a particular series.

Gross Domestic Product in Brief	
Compiled by:	Bureau of Economic Analysis
Frequency:	Quarterly
Release date:	Advance estimate at the end of the first month following the end of the quarter
Revisions:	Two monthly revisions following the advance estimate, annual revisions in July for 3 years, comprehensive revision every 5 years
Published data:	*Economic Indicators*, Council of Economic Advisors
	Survey of Current Business, U.S. Department of Commerce
	THE ECONOMIC BULLETIN BOARD, U.S. Department of Commerce
Hotline update:	(202)606-5306 for a short recorded message

---

[8] Durable goods are generally intended to last more than 3 years.

The Index of Industrial Production

The *index of industrial production* is a comprehensive index of industrial activity compiled by the Board of Governors of the Federal Reserve System, or the Fed. Because of the delays in reporting GDP, the Fed designed the index to give it a quicker reading on the overall health and activity of the manufacturing sector. The index is compiled monthly and released approximately midmonth of the following month.

Industrial Production and GDP

If we break the first-quarter 1994 estimate for GDP down by type of product as in Figure 2-3, we can see that the goods category amounted to 39.6 percent of the total produced. The index of industrial production and each of its subcomponents are based on data collected directly from a number of sources, including gas and electric utilities, the Bureau of Mines, the Bureau of the Census, other government agencies, and industry trade associations. In most cases, the data reflect actual production in the specific industries. In all, approximately 255 individual series representing 26 major industries are used in the index.[9] After the source data are collected, they are compiled and then expressed as a percentage of 1987 output.

Industrial production is usually reported in one of several ways: the first is the *total index*, which is a compilation of all individual indices. For analytical purposes, separate measures for major market groupings and major industry groups are also provided. Further breakdowns of these categories are illustrated in Figure 2.3.

---

[9] Twenty-four of the industries have specific two-digit Standard Industrial Classification (SIC) codes; the remaining two industries are electric and gas utilities.

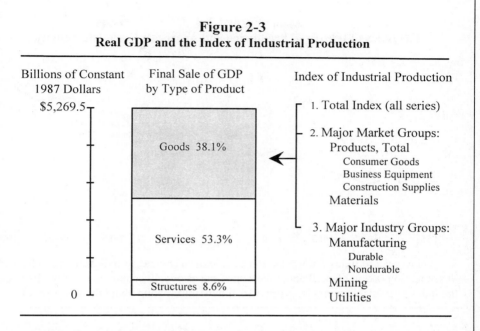

Figure 2-3
Real GDP and the Index of Industrial Production

The index of industrial production is made up of 255 series that track approximately 38 percent of GDP. Coverage includes 26 individual industries, including gas and electric utilities. Breakdowns of the total index are provided for both major market and industry groupings.

What About the Historical Record?

Figure 2-4 shows that the total index of industrial production tends to rise when the economy is expanding and to contract when the economy is in recession. This is to be expected, since the production of durable and nondurable goods represents such a large proportion of overall production. The BEA defines the series as a coincident one, meaning that the peaks and troughs in the series occur at approximately the same time as the economy peaks and troughs.

The durable and nondurable goods components of the index are shown in Figure 2-5. The durable goods portion of the index is usually more

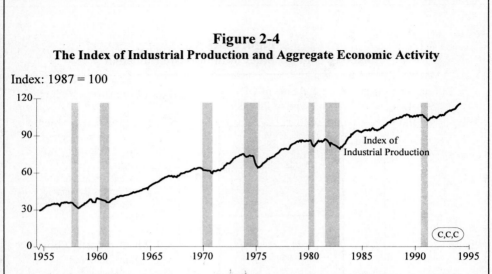

Figure 2-4
The Index of Industrial Production and Aggregate Economic Activity

Index: 1987 = 100

The index of industrial production behaves as a coincident indicator, with changes in production taking place at about the same time as overall economic activity. Because the index is available monthly, it provides timely information about the status of GDP.

volatile since the purchase of durable goods--automobiles, furniture, and appliances--can usually be postponed if consumers find themselves short of cash. The durables index, like the overall index of industrial production, tends to be a coincident indicator with a tendency to plummet during recessionary periods.

Purchases of nondurables--products like food and clothing--are less likely to be postponed, which gives slightly more stability to the index. For this and other reasons, the nondurable goods index acts as a coincident indicator when it comes to peaks in economic activity, and as a leading indicator when it comes to troughs. On an overall basis, the nondurable component of the total index acts as a leading indicator of future economic activity.

The index of industrial production provides a timely and reasonably accurate description of overall industrial production, which accounts for a significant portion of total economic activity. The index does *not* supply

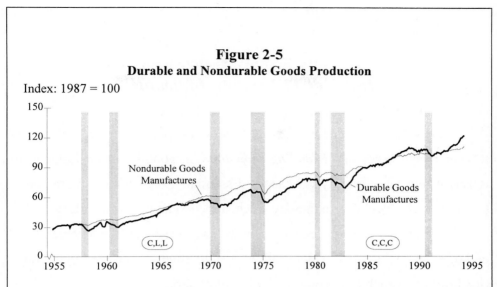

Figure 2-5
Durable and Nondurable Goods Production

Index: 1987 = 100

The durable goods component of the index of industrial production is more volatile than its nondurable counterpart. The nondurable component even serves as a leading indicator when it comes to predicting the end of a recession.

information on services--and so it is not completely descriptive of changes in GDP--but it does provide some of the most comprehensive and timely information available prior to the release of quarterly GDP statistics.

The Index of Industrial Production in Brief

Indicator status:	Coincident with changes in real GDP
Compiled by:	Federal Reserve System Board of Governors
Frequency:	Monthly
Release date:	Preliminary estimate around the fifteenth of the following month
Revisions:	Preliminary estimate subject to revision in each of the subsequent 3 months, annual revision every fall for the previous 2 years, benchmark revision every 5 years
Published data:	*Economic Indicators*, Council of Economic Advisors
	Federal Reserve Bulletin, Federal Reserve Board of Governors
	Statistical Release G.17, Federal Reserve Board of Governors
	Survey of Current Business, U.S. Department of Commerce
	THE ECONOMIC BULLETIN BOARD, U.S. Department of Commerce
Hotline update:	None

Index of 11 Leading Indicators

One of the most interesting, and occasionally controversial, statistics is the composite *index of 11 leading indicators*, a monthly series designed to tell us where the economy is headed. Essentially, the series is a predictive tool to tell us if, and approximately when, a recession might take place.

The series is usually released by the Department of Commerce at the end of every month. It is widely followed and frequently reported in the form of a brief chart such as the one shown in Figure 2-6.

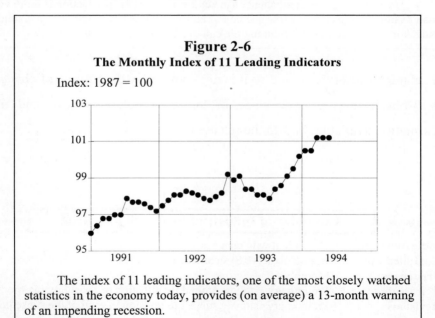

Figure 2-6
The Monthly Index of 11 Leading Indicators

Index: 1987 = 100

The index of 11 leading indicators, one of the most closely watched statistics in the economy today, provides (on average) a 13-month warning of an impending recession.

How Do We Interpret the Index?

In general, most observers focus on changes in the direction of the index. For example, if the index declines for three consecutive months, many observers believe that it has signaled that a recession is about to begin.

In the same way, three consecutive monthly increases are taken as a sign that the economy will prosper or continue to prosper. The most difficult case to interpret is one where the index goes up for several months and then down for several months--or moves in no particular pattern--as it did from mid-1991 to mid-1993.

How Was the Index Developed?

Intuitively, the concept of a leading indicator is fairly easy to grasp. We start with the observation that the overall economy is made up of all types of economic activity. Next we ask, Could it be that some activities take place or that some events occur in *advance* of changes in the overall economy? If so, perhaps we could focus on these activities and use them to predict how the entire economy might behave in the near future.

Back in the 1950s, the National Bureau of Economic Research thought this might be happening, and so they ran thousands of statistical series through their computers and compared the data to changes in real GNP (GDP is now used instead). One set of data examined was an index of stock prices, which (as it turned out) usually declined sharply just before a recession got underway.

Theoretically, the linkage between stock prices and overall spending makes sense. For example, if people feel poorer because of their losses in the market, they might decide to cut back on spending. If enough people feel poorer, their collective decision to spend less may actually affect economic growth.

By itself, however, a measure of stock price performance could not be used as the sole indicator of future economic activity because stock prices sometimes went down while the economy kept going up. Using the approach that there is safety in numbers, why not look for some other statistical series to combine with stock prices?

It turned out that building permits for private housing also behaved somewhat like stock prices--the total number of permits issued tended to decrease several months before the economy turned down. Again, this seems to make sense because a decline in building permits may well mean that a substantial amount of economic activity will either be delayed or not take place at all.

Eventually, the list was narrowed down to a handful and combined in the form of a composite index. The resulting series usually changed direction some months *before* the economy did, hence the term "leading indicator." The index offered considerable promise, and so the Department of Commerce took over the task of collecting and publishing the data. The list of component series in the index (the components change from time to time) is presented in Table 2-4.

Table 2-4
The Index of 11 Leading Indicators, Component Series

1. Average weekly hours of production or nonsupervisory workers in manufacturing
2. Average weekly initial claims for unemployment insurance, state programs (inverted)
3. Manufacturers' new orders for consumer goods and materials, constant 1987 dollars
4. Vendor performance--slower deliveries diffusion index
5. Contracts and orders for plant and equipment in 1987 dollars
6. New private housing authorized by local building permits
7. Change in manufacturers' unfilled orders in 1987 dollars, durable goods, smoothed
8. Change in sensitive materials prices, smoothed
9. Stock prices, 500 common stocks
10. Money supply M2 in 1987 dollars
11. Index of consumer expectations (University of Michigan series)

Source: *Survey of Current Business*, June 1994.

The Historical Record

Most of the controversy concerning the index centers around whether or not three consecutive downturns actually forecast an economic slowdown.

In Figure 2-7, the index of 11 leading indicators has been plotted from 1955 to the present. The shaded areas, as before, represent recessions so that we can compare the turning points of the index with contractions in real GDP.

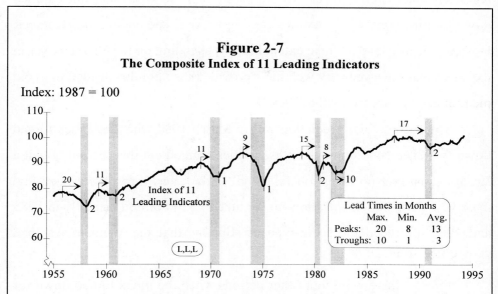

Figure 2-7
The Composite Index of 11 Leading Indicators

Index: 1987 = 100

Lead Times in Months			
	Max.	Min.	Avg.
Peaks:	20	8	13
Troughs:	10	1	3

The index of 11 leading indicators does a much better job predicting the beginning of a recession than the beginning of an expansion. With the exception of the 1981-1982 recession, the average lead time for a trough was so short that the economy was usually well on its way to recovery before the recovery was detected by the leading index.

Figure 2-7 clearly shows that every recession during the last 40 years was preceded by a sharp drop in the composite index of leading indicators. The warnings averaged 13 months and ranged from 8 to 20 months.

Less important, but worth mentioning, is the ability of the index to predict when a recession is about to end. Figure 2-7 shows that the lead time has ranged from 1 to 10 months, with the average closer to 3 months. However, since we cannot identify a turning point in the index until at least 3 months *after* it has actually occurred, the economy is usually well out of the recession before it can be predicted by the index.

Has the Index Ever Failed to Predict a Recession?

Since 1955 the index of leading indicators has twice predicted a recession that never arrived. The first was in 1966 when the index turned down for nine consecutive months starting in April and ending in December. However, heavy (and to some extent hidden) spending on the Vietnam war in the years that followed may well have provided the stimulus needed to avoid the recession predicted by the index.[10]

The second false prediction was in March 1984 when the index turned down for seven consecutive months. Critics pointed out that the index sent a strong signal, yet no recession followed. Advocates, however, argued that massive federal deficit spending--to the tune of $200 billion annually in 1985 and 1986--provided the same type of stimulus that the Vietnam war had earlier.

Finally, there were four other periods when the index turned down for 3 or 4 months and yet a recession did not set in. The first of these occurred in early 1962 when the indicators turned down 3 months in a row. The second occurred in late 1987 when the index turned down 4 months in a row.

The last two instances are evident in Figure 2-6 which shows the indicators turning down for three straight months in late 1991 and 4 months in mid-1992. By mid-1993, however, the index began a series of sharp gains which more than offset the earlier declines.

Do these false calls negate the predictive power or usefulness of the index of leading indicators? Certainly the index is not perfect, and while its usefulness is a topic of debate in some circles, our own view is that even flawed tools are useful so long as we understand their limitations.

---

[10] Most economists exclude wartime periods because of distortion in the domestic statistics. The NBER, for example, compiles separate statistics on the length of peacetime expansions, contractions, and overall business cycles (see Table 2-2 on page 20).

Are There Other Problems with the Index?

Frequent revisions of the monthly numbers are the major source of frustration for analysts.   Whenever a new monthly index number is announced, revisions are also made in the six previous monthly numbers. Every October, revisions are also made for the previous 5 years, which means that the monthly numbers are almost always changing.

For example, there were several periods in 1989 and 1990 when the index turned down 2 months in a row.   Those who believed that a third consecutive decline usually signals a recession watched anxiously for the next release.   Some new releases actually declined, but they were often coupled with upward revisions of earlier (negative) numbers--leaving observers with two *newer* consecutive months of decline--and attention was again riveted on the coming month's figures.

Historically, the index of 11 leading indicators has been one of our most popular forecasting tools. However, it did not do as well in the 1980s, and it issued two false calls shortly after the 1991 recession. The index may have lost some of its luster, but is still one of the main tools in the forecaster's tool kit.

Index of Leading Indicators in Brief

Indicator status:	Leading for recessions, recoveries, and overall
Compiled by:	Bureau of Economic Analysis
Frequency:	Monthly
Release date:	5 weeks after the closing of the survey month
Revisions:	Up to six previous months are revised with every new release.
Published data:	*Economic Indicators*, Council of Economic Advisors
	Survey of Current Business, U.S. Department of Commerce
	THE ECONOMIC BULLETIN BOARD, U.S. Department of Commerce
Hotline update:	(202)606-5361 for a brief recorded message 24 hours a day. The message is updated weekly, usually on Monday, to include new components as they become available.

Purchasing Managers' Index

One of the more interesting indicators of economic activity is the monthly *purchasing managers' index* (*PMI*) compiled by the National Association of Purchasing Management (NAPM).[11] The series is one of a handful of major series maintained by a private industry and/or educational group rather than the U.S. Department of Commerce.[12]

The survey covers manufacturing firms only and examines a number of topics including production, new orders, inventories of purchased materials, employment, and vendor deliveries. The vendor deliveries series is also used by the U.S. Department of Commerce as one of the components in the *index of 11 leading indicators*. The NAPM releases the index in the first week following the close of the reporting month.

The Sample and the Survey

The index is based on a short, 12-question, monthly survey of purchasing managers at over 300 companies in approximately 20 industries. Each industry is weighted according to its contribution to GDP, and each firm in the industry is given equal weight, regardless of its size.[13] The

[11] NAPM is a not-for-profit association of purchasing management executives that specializes in management research and educational materials relating to purchasing, materials management, and business information. The organization has over 36,000 members. For more information, write to NAPM Information Center, P.O. Box 22160, Tempe AZ, 85282-0960 or call (800)888-6276.

[12] Other series examined in this book include the *help-wanted advertising index* and the *consumer confidence survey* compiled by The Conference Board, the *index of consumer expectations* compiled by the Institute for Social Research at the University of Michigan, the *Dow Jones Industrial Average* compiled by the Dow Jones Corporation, and the *S&P 500* compiled by Standard & Poor's Corporation.

[13] Bretz, Robert J., "Behind the Economic Indicators of the NAPM Report on Business," July 1990, in NAPM's *Report on Business Information Kit*, 1994.

questions, such as the one following on vendor deliveries, are unique in that they are designed to detect changes in the level of business activity:[14]

> 9. VENDOR DELIVERIES - Check the **ONE** box that best expresses the current month's **OVERALL** delivery performance compared to the previous month.
>
> ☐ **Faster** than   ☐ **Same** as a   ☐ **Slower** than
>   a month ago   month ago   a month ago

When all of the responses are collected, the results are tabulated and then reported in the form of a diffusion index.

What Does a Diffusion Index Tell Us?

A diffusion index is different from other series in that it focuses on the direction and magnitude of change as opposed to the absolute level of the series.[15] The index ranges from 0 to 100 percent and is considered to be expanding whenever it has a value greater than 50 percent. And the more the number exceeds 50 percent, the more intense the expansion of the series. By the same token, the series is contracting when the index is less than 50 percent, and the contraction is more intense the smaller the number.

In addition to the series on vendor deliveries, separate indices are constructed for production, new orders, inventories of purchased materials, and employment. The five individual series are then combined into the overall purchasing management index.[16]

The Historical Record

Figure 2-8 shows the purchasing manager's index from 1965 to mid-1991. The horizontal line at 44.5 percent is the value of the index thought by

---

[14] Sample questionnaire, NAPM, 1994. NAPM now calls the series "supplier deliveries"; BEA calls it "vendor performance."

[15] To illustrate, weights of 1, 0.5, and 0 are given to each of the three responses above. If half of the respondents select "faster" and if half respond "slower," the index will have a value of 50 percent [or, $0.5(1) + 0.5(0) = 0.5$]. Likewise, if 60 percent respond "faster," 20 percent "same," and 20 percent "slower," the index will have a value of 70 percent [or, $0.6(1) + 0.2(0.5) + 0.2(0) = 0.7$]

[16] The weights vary, with new orders having the most importance.

many to be most consistent with *no change* in real GDP (the economy should be expanding when the index is above 44.5; it should be contracting when the index is below 44.5). The manufacturing sector of the economy is also claimed to be generally expanding when the index is above 50 percent, and contracting when below that level.

Figure 2-8
The Purchasing Managers' Index

Whenever the PMI is greater than 44.5 percent, the overall economy is expanding. Whenever the PMI is over 50 percent, the manufacturing sector of the economy--less than 25 percent of GDP--is expanding. Because the PMI is based on a weighted average of five separate diffusion indices, the overall index has the properties of a leading indicator-- reaching a peak before the economy peaks and a trough before the economy troughs.

According to the figure, the economy indeed expanded when the index exceeded 44.5 percent. At the same time, however, we should note that the index was in excess of 44.5 percent *most* of the time--including the recessionary periods in 1970, 1974, and some of 1980. Accordingly, we have to be careful to avoid the use of simplistic rules when evaluating the series.

Instead, it helps to examine the intensity of change as well as the general direction. For example, when the index was above 44.5 percent and *rising*, as in late 1958, 1961, 1971, 1975-1976, 1981, and 1983, the economy was indeed expanding. Yet, when the index was above 40 and declining, the economy tended to slow down and eventually entered a recession, as in the early part of 1956, all of 1959, the late 1960s, 1973-1974, 1978-1979, and 1988-1990.

Because the PMI is a diffusion index, it has the properties of a leading indicator. If we examine Figure 2-8, we can see that the index peaked well in advance of the impending recession (with a highly variable lead time). Likewise, the index usually hit a minimum just before, or about the same time as, the recovery began. Since the BEA does not venture a leading or lagging classification for the series, we are left to our own judgments.[17] It seems, however, as if the series tends to be a leading indicator for recessions and a leading or coincident indicator for recoveries.[18]

The Purchasing Managers' Index in Brief

Indicator status:	The level of the PMI is a coincident indicator; peaks and troughs in the PMI series function more as a leading indicator
Compiled by:	National Association of Purchasing Management
Frequency:	Monthly
Release date:	First week following the reporting month
Revisions:	None; responses are raw data and are not changed
Published data:	*Report on Business*, a monthly NAPM journal
	THE ECONOMIC BULLETIN BOARD, U.S. Department of Commerce
Hotline update:	None

---

[17] The peak in the series is analogous to an inflection point in a series that grows first at an increasing and then at a decreasing rate. The trough is analogous to an inflection point for a series that decreases at an increasing and then at a decreasing rate.

[18] A 1985 paper presented by Theodore S. Torda at the NAPM International Conference and later published in *Purchasing Management* (July 1985, pp. 20-22) states that ". . . monthly data on the NAPM composite index and the Commerce Department's composite of leading economic indicators . . . (both) tend to reach their peaks and troughs before those of the general business cycle." Later in the same paper, the author states that "the NAPM composite index clearly leads the (BEA) coincident index."

Another paper by Alan Raedels, "Forecasting the NAPM Purchasing Managers' Index," in the *Journal of Purchasing and Materials Management* (Fall 1990), concluded that "the Purchasing Manager's Index can be considered a coincident indicator of the economy."

Labor Productivity

The key measure of labor efficiency in the U.S. economy is labor productivity, also called worker productivity. The series for all workers is called *output per hour for all persons, business sector* and is compiled quarterly by the Bureau of Labor Statistics with a base year of 1982 = 100.[19]

The series is widely regarded as a measure of efficiency, but it has little value as an indicator of future economic activity because it is compiled using quarterly output.

How Do We Measure Productivity?

Officially, the BLS defines the measure as:

$$\text{Labor productivity} = \frac{\text{constant dollar output}}{\text{hours of labor input}}$$

The numerator is essentially the same as, and is based on, the GDP statistics in national income and product accounts. The numerator is measured in real terms so that prices do not distort the output (goods and services) actually produced. The denominator is obtained from monthly data on total employment from the BLS Current Employment Statistics (CES) program which provides monthly survey data on payrolls in various industries.[20]

The Historical Record

The historical index, shown in Figure 2-9, indicates that labor productivity has grown slowly but steadily since 1955. The index reached

---

[19] The BLS also compiles a second series, *output per hour, all persons, nonfarm business sector* which excludes the farm sector.
[20] *BLS Handbook of Methods*, Bulletin 2414, pp. 89-90.

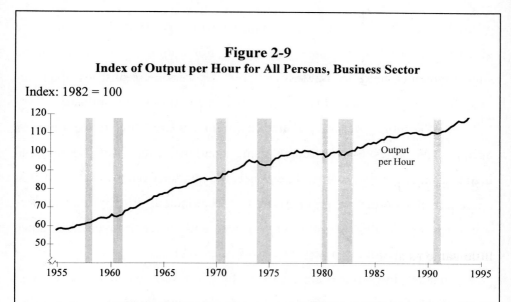

Figure 2-9
Index of Output per Hour for All Persons, Business Sector

Index: 1982 = 100

Labor productivity is defined as the amount of constant dollar output produced per hour. It is an important economic measure, but not well suited to the prediction of short-term economic activity because it is derived from quarterly data.

119.8 in the first quarter of 1994, meaning that workers produced 19.8 percent more output per hour than they did in 1982. When farm workers are removed from the sample, the index slips to 117.8, which indicates relatively lower productivity in manufacturing than in agriculture.

The index also exhibits some cyclical behavior, with productivity falling off at the end of the expansion--most likely because employers tend to hire less skilled and therefore less productive workers when production is high and unemployment rates are low. When the recession sets in, these workers are usually the first to go and productivity picks up again.

What Else Should We Know about Labor Productivity?

Several things. For one, labor productivity ignores the capital goods (tools and machinery) used by the workers. Because of this, any change in the quantity or quality of capital goods used can affect the measure. For example, worker productivity in an industry would go up if all workers were given more efficient equipment to use.[21]   For another, the index and its subcomponents tend to be less reliable for service industries than for manufacturing since output is harder to measure in the service industry.

Furthermore, worker productivity numbers are slow to be reported because the series is constructed using quarterly data from the national income and product accounts. In essence, the quarterly output data must first be generated in order for productivity to be computed. Finally, the series is useful when analyzing long-term price and wage movements since productivity is required to keep price increases in check.

In short, the series is extremely useful if we want to examine or explain some of the factors that contribute to long-term economic growth. Worker productivity is a long-term trend measure and should be evaluated from this perspective.[22]

Labor Productivity in Brief

Indicator status:	None
Compiled by:	Bureau of Labor Statistics
Frequency:	Quarterly
Release date:	30 days after the close of the quarter
Revisions:	First revisions 30 days after the initial release, additional revision 60 days after initial release, final revision announced with release of next quarter estimates
Published Data:	*Economic Indicators*, Council of Economic Advisors
	Monthly Labor Review, U.S. Department of Labor
	Survey of Current Business, U.S. Department of Commerce
	THE ECONOMIC BULLETIN BOARD, U.S. Department of Commerce
Hotline update:	None

---

[21] The BLS computes a multifactor productivity series for major industry sectors that uses both labor *and* capital in the denominator. This measure is not followed in the press--although it should be!

[22] The BLS compiles several other productivity measures, but only the ones discussed here are published regularly in the *Survey of Current Business*. See Chapters 10 and 11 in the *BLS Handbook of Methods*, Bulletin 2414, for other measures.

Capacity Utilization

When the Federal Reserve System collects data on industrial production, it also makes estimates of manufacturing capacity. The *capacity utilization rate, manufacturing* is the ratio of industrial production to capacity. Estimates of industrial capacity are available for a number of industries and product groups, including manufacturing, mining, utilities, durable goods, chemicals, and paper, to name a few. The monthly series is released approximately 2 weeks after the close of the month.

Why Is Capacity Important to the Fed?

One of the responsibilities of the Fed is to foster steady economic growth in a climate of reasonable price stability. The capacity utilization rate is designed to tell the Fed if the economy is "heating up" to the point where inflation might surge because of bottlenecks in production. This sometimes happens when demand for output is so strong that producers are tempted to use less skilled labor and less efficient equipment to generate even more output.

This makes the series a little different in that it is not exclusively intended to forecast changes in future economic activity. Instead, the series is designed as a guide to monetary policy. When the capacity utilization rate gets too high, the Fed might be tempted to tighten the money supply to slow the economy and lessen the potential threat of inflation. When the capacity utilization rate is lower, the economy is perceived to have some "slack" that acts to ease inflationary pressures.

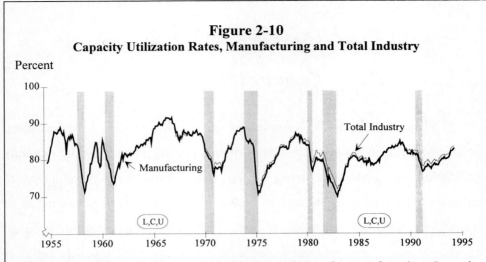

Figure 2-10
Capacity Utilization Rates, Manufacturing and Total Industry

Originally, the Fed made capacity utilization estimates for manufacturing. Later, it it added mining, utilities, and several others to get a "total industry" series which is now available from 1967 to the present. Despite the availability of the separate "total" series, manufacturing gets most of the attention.

What About the Historical Record?

The capacity utilization rates for manufacturing and total industry are shown in Figure 2-10. Because the series are expressed as a percent of capacity, the level never exceeds 100. The BEA classifies both as leading indicators for peaks. Unfortunately, the lead time is too variable to be of much value for forecasting. Overall, they have unclassified indicator status.

Capacity Utilization in Brief	
Indicator status:	Leading for recessions, coincident for recoveries
Compiled by:	Federal Reserve System Board of Governors
Frequency:	Monthly
Release date:	Preliminary estimate made midmonth of the following month
Revisions:	The preliminary estimate is revised for up to 3 months; annual revisions are targeted for fall, benchmark revisions every 5 years
Published data:	*Economic Indicators*, Council of Economic Advisors
	Federal Reserve Bulletin, Federal Reserve Board of Governors
	Statistical Release G.17, Federal Reserve Board of Governors
	Survey of Current Business, U.S. Department of Commerce
	THE ECONOMIC BULLETIN BOARD, U.S. Department of Commerce
Hotline update:	None

Chapter 3

INVESTMENT AND CAPITAL EXPENDITURES

Gross Private Nonresidential Fixed Investment

In the first quarter of 1994, business sector expenditures, also known as *gross private domestic investment*, accounted for 14.6 percent of total GDP.[1] The majority of these expenditures were for nonresidential structures and producers' durable equipment. Several series were constructed to monitor these expenditures, but two stand out: **gross private nonresidential fixed investment,** and **new plant and equipment expenditures.**[2]

Neither series classifies as a leading indicator, and one is even being replaced--so why are they important? The answer is rooted in the long search for stable and predictable relationships in economics.

The Search for Stable Relationships

When Keynes wrote his magnificent *General Theory of Employment, Interest, and Money* during the Great Depression of the 1930s, he offered a bold and radical explanation as to how the economy functioned.[3] His approach was based on a conceptual framework that broke the economy

---

[1] The breakdown for the first quarter of 1994 is shown in Table 3-1 and Table 2-3 on page 22.
[2] Others are the *index of net business formation*, the *number of new business incorporations, the index of industrial production, business equipment* (a subset of the Fed's *index of industrial production*), and several small series covering contracts, orders, and other business commitments.
[3] John Maynard Keynes, *The General Theory of Employment, Interest, and Money*, Harcourt, Brace & Co., New York, 1936.

down into sectors and then described, in considerable detail, the spending behavior of each.   Among other things, he argued that spending by the consumer sector was relatively stable.

This was extremely important because if it could be shown that the greater part of total economic activity (consumer spending) behaved in a stable and predictable manner, the instability of the total economy could be traced to other, and smaller, components--specifically spending by the business sector.

However, there were no GDP statistics that could be used to verify his convictions.   Nevertheless, his description of spending by each sector was so detailed that academicians started collecting data to test his theories.   In the end, research largely confirmed the propositions put forth in the *General Theory*.   Before long, the data grew into the NIPA accounts that feature the GDP, GNP, NNP, and other measures of aggregate economic performance that we use today.   These accounts, along with the organization of Tables 2-3 and 3-1, and numerous other tables and figures used throughout this book, are directly descended from Keynes' work.

Table 3-1 illustrates the stability of spending by the various sectors of the economy.   The table follows the format of Table 2-3, only this time the focus is on quarterly percentage changes of GDP components over time.   In the first quarter of 1994, personal consumption expenditures amounted to 68.9 percent of GDP.   In addition, 14.6 percent was consumed by the business sector, -1.3 percent was consumed by the foreign sector, and 17.7 percent was consumed by the government sector.

Columns 2 and 3 show the range of percentage changes for each category, with the average percentage change shown in the fourth column. The standard deviation (a measure of dispersion) appears next, while the coefficient of variation (a measure of relative dispersion) appears in the last column.

Even the most casual inspection of the table reveals the stability of the consumer sector and the relative instability of the business (or investment) sector that was predicted by Keynes.[4] This instability should be enough to make it worthy of study--but there's more. Investment sector expenditures, again described by Keynes, have a way of causing *additional* expenditures through the multiplier principle.[5]

Table 3-1
Quarterly Percentage Changes in GDP Components, 1954-1994

	% GDP in 1994-I	Maximum Change	Minimum Change	Mean Change	Standard Deviation	CV
Gross domestic product	*100.0*	*5.9%*	*-1.6%*	*1.8%*	*1.1%*	*0.59*
*Personal consumption expenditures**	*68.9*	*4.3%*	*-0.1%*	*1.9%*	*0.8%*	*0.42*
Durable goods	8.7	12.8%	-9.4%	1.9%	3.5%	1.85
Nondurable goods	20.9	4.1%	-0.7%	1.6%	0.9%	0.59
Services	39.3	3.8%	0.7%	2.2%	0.6%	0.28
Gross private domestic investment†	*14.6*	*14.6%*	*-15.4%*	*2.0%*	*5.2%*	*2.63*
Fixed investment	14.3	9.2%	-7.17%	1.8%	2.6%	1.39
Nonresidential	10.1	9.9%	-8.2%	1.9%	2.6%	1.37
Residential	4.2	15.5%	-17.4%	1.8%	5.2%	2.83
Change in business inventories	0.3	3,450.0%	-2,415.0%	-8.6%	474.0%	55.12
Net exports of goods and services‡	*-1.3*	*11.0%*	*-7.0%*	*2.6%*	*166.2%*	*64.45*
Exports	10.2	10.3%	-10.9%	2.5%	4.6%	1.81
Import	11.5	20.3%	-9.1%	2.6%	4.3%	1.67
Govt. purchases of goods, services§	*17.7*	*5.4%*	*-3.4%*	*1.7%*	*1.4%*	*0.80*
Federal	6.7	7.6%	-6.3%	1.4%	2.5%	1.73
State and local	11.1	4.5%	-0.2%	2.2%	0.9%	0.44

*Consumer sector.
†Business sector.
‡Foreign Sector.
§Government sector.
Note: The numerical size of the standard deviation is sometimes difficult to interpret because series with relatively large means tend to have larger standard deviations. To compensate, we can compute a coefficient of variation (CV) which is the standard deviation divided by the mean--thereby making comparisons of two series with different means possible. Here a CV of 0.42 for personal consumption expenditures tells us that quarterly percentage changes for this sector are one of the most stable in the table. Likewise, a CV of 2.63 for gross private domestic investment means that quarterly percentage changes in this series are roughly 6 times (2.63/.42 = 6.3) more volatile than personal consumption expenditures.

---

[4] The net foreign sector is the least stable of all, with a CV of 64.45, but it is also relatively small.
[5] The multiplier is defined as the change in overall spending caused by a change in investment spending. The President's Council of Economic Advisors has estimated that the multiplier for the United States economy is about 2. This means that $1 billion of investment spending will ultimately generate $2 billion of total output.

The Historical Record

Both of the capital investment series plotted in Figure 3-1 give us a feel for the instability of business sector spending. This instability is especially evident when the figure is compared to consumer spending in Figure 5-1 on page 79. For example, nonresidential fixed investment in constant dollars peaked in the third quarter of 1990, and then dropped 8.2 percent over the next five quarters. During the same period, constant dollar spending by the consumer sector dropped a scant 0.65 percent.

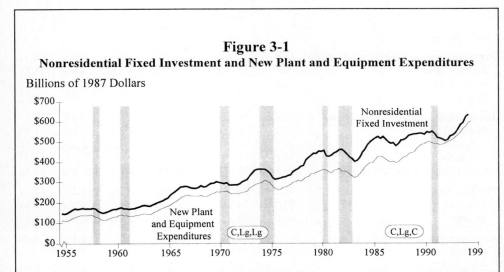

Figure 3-1
Nonresidential Fixed Investment and New Plant and Equipment Expenditures

Expenditures by business tend to turn down when the economy turns down, and up only after the economy has recovered. These changes have a magnified effect on the economy because of the multiplier effect. New plant and equipment expenditures were not benchmarked after 1982, and the series was discontinued in 1994.

Make Way for ACES

Note that we haven't said much about new plant and equipment expenditures series, even though it is displayed in Figure 3-1. The reason is this series was no longer published after the second quarter of 1994. It turned out that the series was less useful than previously thought.

Basically, data concerning *planned* capital expenditures were collected quarterly by means of a mail questionnaire that was sent out to a scientifically selected sample of business firms in 39 industries. At the beginning of the year, firms would report their plans for first-quarter spending. If these plans were delayed, some respondents would simply push the planned expenditures ahead to the next quarter. When the last quarter arrived, however, there was a tendency for firms to simply cancel the delayed expenditures altogether, thus causing distortions in the quarterly figures.

To make matters worse, benchmark revisions that were normally done every 5 years or so to assure the validity of the sample were not conducted after 1982! As a result, the series became less and less reliable with respect to the *level* of capital expenditures, although there was less concern with the timing of the turning points.

Eventually the level of planned plant and equipment expenditures did not track well with nonresidential fixed investment, so the Department of Commerce decided to replace it with a new semiannual series based on its Annual Capital Expenditures Survey (ACES).[6] At the time of this writing, the name of the new series had not been determined, although it is expected to cover 14 industry groups and be published in February and September.

Gross Private Nonresidential Fixed Investment	
Indicator status:	Coincident for recessions, lagging for recoveries, coincident overall
Compiled by:	Bureau of Economic Analysis
Frequency:	Quarterly
Release date:	End of the month with GDP revisions
Revisions:	Advance, revised, and final revisions along with GDP revisions
Published data:	*Economic Indicators*, Council of Economic Advisors
	Survey of Current Business, U.S. Department of Commerce
	THE ECONOMIC BULLETIN BOARD, U.S. Department of Commerce
Hotline update:	None

---

[6] Data users are not very excited about a semiannual series, but the Department of Commerce feels that this will force the firms in the sample to reevaluate planned capital expenditures earlier, rather than let them slide as they often did with the new plant and equipment series.

Building Permits and Housing Starts

Residential construction amounted to 4.2 percent of total GDP in the first quarter of 1994. This may not seem like a relatively large part of overall economic activity, but the multiplier effect causes housing expenditures to have an amplified impact on the economy. Several series are used to track housing activity, but the two that receive the most attention in the press will be discussed here: an index of new building permits issued, and statistics on the number of new homes started.[7]

The first is officially known as ***new private housing units authorized by local building permits***--which explains the more common and considerably shorter title. Building permits is also the only housing series included in the composite *index of 11 leading indicators*.[8] The second measure is the ***new private housing units started*** series. This differs from new building permits in that it represents actual home-building activity, not just the intention to build.

Do Building Permits Predict Future Economic Activity?

On one level, the relationship between new building permits issued and overall economic activity may seem tenuous. In the first place, a building permit represents the *intention* to spend rather than a commitment to spend. The permit is also relatively inexpensive to obtain and is sometimes acquired

---

[7] Two others are *gross private residential fixed investment* in constant dollars and the Department of Housing and Urban Development's (HUD) series on the sales of new homes. The former tracks the housing component of the NIPA accounts and is reported quarterly. The latter reports total dollar sales rather than thousands of units as is the case of housing starts.

[8] The preliminary release, on a seasonally adjusted annual basis, is available on the twelfth workday of every month and is the one reported in the press. The final figures for the series are available on the eighteenth and are the ones included in the *index of 11 leading indicators*.

partially for precautionary reasons, for example, "in case" the opportunity to build is right. In addition, the amount of time between issuance of the permit and the start of the new residence may vary greatly from one location to another.

Finally, the intent to build may be adversely affected by changes in interest rates after the permit is issued. In short, there are several reasons why the number of building permits issued might not work very well as an economic indicator.

The Historical Record

But work well they do. As can be seen in Figure 3-2, the index of new private building permits tends to increase sharply during economic expansions and then decline sharply some months before the expansion ends and/or the recession begins. Even before the recession has ended, the index begins to shoot up dramatically, foretelling the impending recovery.

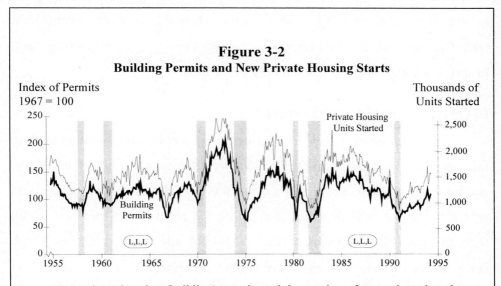

Figure 3-2
Building Permits and New Private Housing Starts

New private housing (building) permits and the number of new private housing units started both function as leading indicators for impending recessions and recoveries. The main problem with both series is the relative size of the month-to-month variations which can obscure the underlying trend.

Figure 3-2 also illustrates the size of the swings in the index. For example, it is not unusual for the index to double in a very short time, as it did right after 1970, 1975, and 1982. The sharp rise in January 1990 appeared to indicate that the economy would perk up again--when it was actually about to enter a recession. As a result, we have to interpret the sudden and often sharp movements in the building permit index with care.

What About Housing Starts?

This series differs from building permits in that it is expressed in terms of thousands of private houses started annually rather than being indexed to a base year. Monthly changes in the series are also volatile--often reaching double-digit levels--but no more so than the index of building permits.[9]

To illustrate, housing starts *jumped* 14.7 percent in December 1993 and then *dropped* 21.2 percent in January 1994. Weather is often the cause of such changes. Since builders usually have a backlog of building permits to use, they tend to break ground early when the weather permits and postpone starts when the weather is inclement--thereby causing housing starts to shift back and forth from one month to the next.

Is One Preferable to the Other?

The good news is that both series function reasonably well as leading indicators for both peaks and troughs in overall economic activity economy. As far as the peaks are concerned, Figure 3-2 clearly shows severe and protracted drops in both series just before the recessionary periods. And, with the possible exception of the 1973-1974 and 1980 recessions, both series turned up before the economy began to recover.

---

[9] The average monthly change (without regard to sign) in the building permits index was 5.2 percent from 1980 until the first quarter of 1994. The average monthly absolute change for new housing starts was 6.6 percent. The coefficient of variation (CV) was 23.7 for permits and 23.4 for starts, so there was little relative difference in variability between the two series for the period.

The bad news is that the housing start series is so volatile that monthly revisions often include changes in the *direction* of movement as well as magnitude.[10] As a result, the monthly housing numbers sometime seem better suited for commentary and speculation than for forecasting changes in future economic activity. You can just imagine the excitement caused by the January 1990 figures for both series which seemed to indicate that the economy was about to perk up again--when in fact it was about to enter a recession.

The main problem with building permits and housing starts is one of interpretation: too often people seem to focus on the size of the monthly change rather than on the underlying trend which make take several months to establish. Both series are revised extensively for several months after the preliminary release, so the trend can be established--it just takes a little longer.

Building Permits and Housing Starts in Brief

Indicator status:	Both series: leading for recessions, recoveries, and overall
Compiled by:	Bureau of the Census
Frequency:	Monthly
Release date:	Preliminary (both series): twelfth workday of the month
	Final (both series): eighteenth workday of the month
Revisions:	Building permits: previous two months revised monthly, annual revision every April
	Housing starts: previous two months revised monthly, annual revision every January
Published data:	*Economic Indicators*, Council of Economic Advisors
	Survey of Current Business, U.S. Department of Commerce
	THE ECONOMIC BULLETIN BOARD, U.S. Department of Commerce
Hotline update:	Because building permits are a component of the *Index of Leading Indicators*, the 3- to 5-minute leading indicator message at (202)606-5361 includes an update of the series when it is updated.

---

[10] Housing starts figures are released along with 90 percent confidence intervals. For example, the June 1994 press release stated that May housing starts were up 3 percent over April, plus or minus 6 percent. In other words, there was a 90 percent chance that housing starts in May were 3 percent *lower* to 9 percent *higher* than in April. Because the range included 0, the change was not statistically significant--and so we are uncertain as to whether there actually was an increase.

Business Inventories

Historically, inventories have played an important role in the literature on recessions and expansions.[11] In general, high inventories have been singled out as contributing to the cause of recessions, while low inventories are sometimes thought to be a sign that business activity is about to pick up. To see how this might come about, let's take a simplistic look at the process.

How Do Inventory Levels Affect Economic Activity?

First, it helps to think of inventories as being a buffer between production and sales. Now suppose that, for some reason, consumers cut back on their spending. The result is likely to be levels of unsold inventories in excess of what businesses would like to carry. If businesses react by reducing orders from suppliers, closing plants, and/or otherwise cutting back on manufacturing, workers will either work shorter hours or lose their jobs.

This, in turn, reduces the amount of income workers have to spend, which may actually cause inventory levels to *increase* again, rather than decrease as businesses had planned. If the cycle repeats itself, production will again fall, employment will dip, and consumer spending will drop, all of which may put the economy on the path to recession.

Eventually, businesses may succeed in reducing production to the point where inventories *are*, in fact, low. If they overshoot their mark, or if consumer spending increases even slightly, inventory shortages may develop.

---

[11] W.S. Jevons, Wesley Mitchell, and John Maynard Keynes were but a few of the many economists to incorporate the role of inventories into their view of the causes and explanations of economic fluctuations. In the late 1940s, Moses Abramovitz's classic work, *The Role of Inventories in Business Cycles*, was published by the National Bureau of Economic Research and did much to influence the way inventory statistics are compiled and reported today.

Businesses will then need to hire more instead of fewer workers. This increases employment and consumer spending, causing inventories to go down again rather than up. As long as businesses continue to try to replenish inventories, the process of playing catch-up helps pull the economy out of recession and puts it on the path to recovery.

But Does It Really Work Like That?

The historical record may provide some clues. In Figure 3-3, the level of business inventories is plotted against economic activity since 1955.

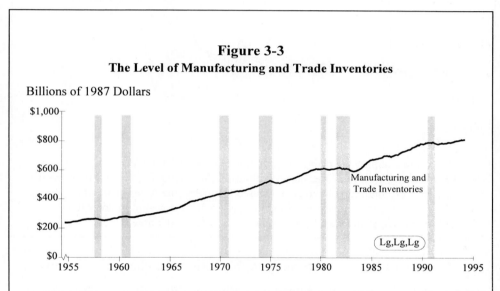

Figure 3-3
The Level of Manufacturing and Trade Inventories

Monthly reports on the *level* of business inventories are widely reported in the press even though most series that report on the dollar amount of inventories tend to be lagging indicators. Lagging indicators are of little value in predicting the direction of future economic activity.

Not very interesting, is it? In fact, any series that reports on the *level* of inventories usually tends to be more of a lagging, not a leading, indicator.[12] This means that inventory levels go up during the expansion and continue to

---

[12] Another popular inventory series is the *ratio, manufacturing and trade inventories to sales in 1987 dollars* measure which also has lagging indicator properties.

rise right on into the recession. Eventually inventory levels may turn down, but not until the recession is about over.

Let's try again. This time (Figure 3-4) we will look at the *change* in the level of inventories rather than at the level itself.

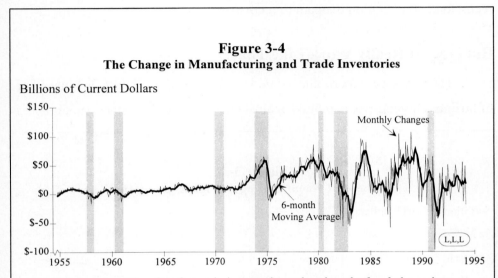

Figure 3-4
The Change in Manufacturing and Trade Inventories

Billions of Current Dollars

When we examine the *change* in inventories rather than the *level*, the series becomes a leading indicator. Because month-to-month fluctuations can easily exceed $100 billion, a 6-month moving average is used to smooth the series. Note that the series does not have to predict every single recession and expansion in order to be classified as a leading indicator--it just has to work most of the time.

That looks better! According to this series, the change in the level of inventories looks more like a leading indicator although it is fairly volatile from one month to the next. That is, the index usually turns down before the economy turns down and usually turns up before the economy turns up.

So Why Even Bother with Inventory Levels?

Because others do! In fact, a number of financial writers insist on reporting the level of business inventories even though it is not helpful as an indicator of *future* economic activity. We still see features on the level of manufacturing inventories (a subset of the series used in Figure 3-3) even though changes in the level are preferable. In addition, such reports often cite the series in current (inflation biased), not constant, dollars.[13] When this happens, the monthly series just goes up.

What Should We Remember about Inventory Statistics?

First, whenever possible, use a series measured in constant dollars to avoid the distortions caused by inflation. For example, the series used for Figure 3-4 is in current dollars, which partially explains the ever-widening monthly fluctuations. If we wanted an index that showed changes in real, or constant, dollars, we would have to settle for quarterly data.

Second, series that track inventory levels are not much help in forecasting future economic activity since they tend to act as lagging indicators. Third, series on changes in the level of inventories tend to act as leading indicators and are most useful for forecasting changes in future economic activity. Finally, if the forecast is for GDP, the choice between manufacturing and trade inventories or simply business inventories is not critical since they all behave about the same.

Change in Manufacturing and Trade Inventories in Brief

Indicator status:	Leading for recessions, recoveries, and overall
Compiled by:	Bureau of Economic Analysis and Bureau of the Census
Frequency:	Monthly
Release date:	Second week of the following month
Revisions:	3 times every quarter as GDP is revised; annual revision in July for the previous 3 years
Published data:	*Economic Indicators*, Council of Economic Advisors
	Survey of Current Business, U.S. Department of Commerce
	THE ECONOMIC BULLETIN BOARD, U.S. Department of Commerce
Hotline update:	None

---

[13] Unfortunately, the first release of numbers from any agency in the Department of Commerce is usually on a current dollar basis. This happens because the price index series used to convert current dollars to inflation-adjusted (or real) dollars is not immediately available.

Durable Goods Orders

Durable goods constitute such an important part of the overall economy, accounting for approximately 9 percent of total GDP, that separate statistics are often kept on this category.[14] We must be careful to distinguish, however, between those durables that are intended for the consumer sector and those intended for use by the business sector.

The series called ***manufacturers' new orders, durable goods industries*** is a measure of the durable goods intended for the business sector.[15] This statistic, representing less than 3 percent of total GDP, is compiled monthly from survey data gathered from approximately 1,700 businesses and is released about 3 weeks after the end of the month.

How Do Durable Goods *Orders* Differ from *Production*?

There are several important differences. First, there is the difference in coverage mentioned above, with the series on durable goods orders representing a much smaller portion of GDP. Second, the Federal Reserve System collects data on the production of all durables, whereas the Bureau of Economic Analysis and the Bureau of the Census (both part of the U.S. Department of Commerce) collect data on durable goods orders.

Third, data on durable goods orders are reported in billions of dollars rather than in the form of an index. The series is available in terms of both current dollars (using prices prevailing at the time the statistic was compiled) and constant 1987 dollars. For the most part, the series in constant dollars,

---

[14] From 1954 until the first quarter of 1994, spending on durable goods ranged from 7.2 to 9.9 percent of total GDP.
[15] This series is often confused with another index, *manufacturers' new orders, consumer goods and materials industries*, which is one of the key components of the *index of 11 leading indicators*.

shown in Figure 3-5, is the more useful of the two because the distortions of inflation have been removed.

Figure 3-5
Manufacturers' New Orders, Durable Goods

New orders for durable goods may have leading indicator status, but the monthly numbers are so volatile that it is sometimes difficult to identify relative peaks and troughs. For the period shown in this figure, the monthly series declined 224 times and increased 255 times!

Just How Useful Is the Series?

Overall, the series gives an uneven performance as a leading indicator because it is fairly volatile in the short run. For the period covered in Figure 3-5, there were 224 monthly declines and 255 monthly increases. In the 37 months shown since the end of the 1990-1991 recession, the series changed direction 23 times! In addition, some of the monthly changes were quite dramatic.

In November 1992, for example, the level of durable goods orders amounted to $107.98 billion in 1987 dollars. In December it increased to $117.64 billion, an increase of 8.9 percent for just one month. In January it dropped to $114.64 billion, for a 2.6 percent decline, and then promptly increased 2.2 percent the month after that.

Whenever a statistical series exhibits this much volatility, it is difficult to infer much from the monthly changes. It is more useful when looked at over a longer period of time, and it may be better to use a moving average to smooth out the short-term changes.

Unfortunately, large changes in any statistical series can capture the attention of the press, and too much is often made of it. This is especially true when most of the economic indicators are giving mixed signals--a combination of events that encourages people to look for more significance in a particular series than is warranted.

Overall, the durable goods orders series is classified as a leading indicator by the Bureau of Economic Analysis. It tends to peak before the economy peaks and to bottom out before the economy bottoms out. However, the variability of the lead times, along with the number and size of the monthly changes, means that this indicator of future economic activity should be used with caution.

New Durable Goods Orders in Brief

Indicator status:	Leading for recessions, recoveries, and overall economic activity
Compiled by:	U.S. Department of Commerce
Frequency:	Monthly
Release date:	Third or fourth week following the end of the month
Revisions:	Monthly revisions to the beginning of the quarter, annual revisions in the Spring, benchmarks every 5 years
Published data:	*Economic Indicators*, Council of Economic Advisors
	Survey of Current Business, U.S. Department of Commerce
	THE ECONOMIC BULLETIN BOARD, U.S. Department of Commerce
Hotline update:	None

Chapter 4

EMPLOYMENT, EARNINGS, AND PROFITS

The Unemployment Rate

Unemployment numbers, specifically the ***civilian unemployment rate***, or simply the ***unemployment rate***, are among the most widely watched of all economic statistics. The rate can move as much as one or two percentage points in a short time, but it has remained within a much smaller range since the Great Depression of the 1930s when it peaked at nearly 25 percent.

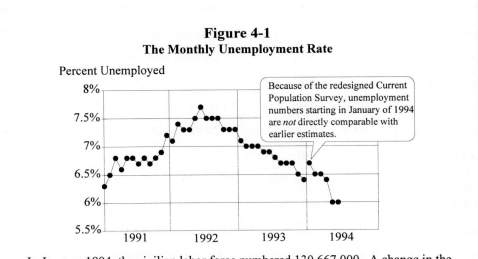

Figure 4-1
The Monthly Unemployment Rate

Percent Unemployed

Because of the redesigned Current Population Survey, unemployment numbers starting in January of 1994 are *not* directly comparable with earlier estimates.

In January 1994, the civilian labor force numbered 130,667,000. A change in the monthly unemployment rate as small as *one-tenth of 1 percent* meant that 130,667 people either lost their jobs or found new ones. Unemployment numbers starting in January 1994 are approximately 0.5 to 0.6 percent *higher* than earlier numbers because of the new survey methods used by the Bureau of Labor Statistics.

How Are the Data Collected?

Unemployment data are collected monthly by the Bureau of the Census for the Bureau of Labor Statistics (BLS) using a survey covering 60,000 households in approximately 2,000 counties and independent cities, with coverage in all 50 states and the District of Columbia. The survey is called the Current Population Survey (CPS), and it is the source of most labor market data, including earnings differentials among worker groups, labor force participation rates, and demographic characteristics of workers.

For consistency, the CPS is conducted in the week containing the nineteenth day of the month, with most questions relating to the week of the twelfth day of the month. The BLS then compiles the data and usually issues labor force information on the first Friday of the following month.

Updating the Current Population Survey

From 1967 to 1993, the questionnaire for the CPS remained essentially unchanged. During that time, however, a number of changes in the economy such as the growth of service jobs, the decline of factory jobs, the more prominent role of women, and the proliferation of alternative work schedules, took place. As a result, the Census Bureau introduced a revised questionnaire in January 1994. The new questions were designed to be easier to understand, to yield more accurate information, and to allow a switch to a more automated interview format.

Sample questions from the old and new survey forms are shown in Figure 4-2.[1] Under the old format, the interviewer had to select the next question based on the answer given to the previous question. Under the new format, each of the 1,500 Census Bureau interviewers uses a portable computer that automatically selects the next question for them.

---

[1] The questions in Figure 4-2 are from *Briefing Materials on the Redesigned Current Population Survey*, by the Bureau of Labor Statistics staff, February 4, 1994. These questions highlight the main differences in the new CPS, but have different numbers on the actual questionnaire.

Figure 4-2
Current Population Survey--Selected Employment and Unemployment Questions

Old CPS	Revised CPS

Revised CPS

1. Does anyone in this household have a business or a farm?

Old CPS

1. What were you doing most of LAST WEEK-
(working or something else?)
(keeping house or something else?)
(going to school or something else?)
If answer indicates "with a job, but not at work" (either temporarily or or on layoff), ask 2, and if 2 is "no" ask 4. If answer indicates "working," skip 2. All others, ask 2.

2. LAST WEEK, did you do ANY work for (either) pay (or profit)?
If 1 is "yes" and 2 is "no," ask 3.

3. LAST WEEK, did you do any unpaid work in the family business or farm?
If 2 and 3 are both "no," ask 4.

2. Did you do any work at all LAST WEEK, not counting work around the house? (Note: If farm or business operator in household, ask about unpaid work.)

4. LAST WEEK (in addition to the business), did you have a job, either full- or part-time? Include any job from which you were temporarily absent.
If 4 is "no," ask 5.

3. Did you have a job or business from which you were temporarily absent or on layoff LAST WEEK?

If "no," ask 5. If "yes," ask 4.

5. LAST WEEK, were you on layoff from a job?
If 5 is "yes," ask 6. If 5 is "no," ask 8.

4. Why were you absent from work LAST WEEK?

6. Has your employer given you a date to return to work?
If "no," ask 7.

7. Have you been given any indication that you will be recalled to work within the next 6 months?
If "no," ask 8.

5. Have you been looking for work during the past 4 weeks?
If "yes," ask 6

8. Have you been doing anything to find work during the last 4 weeks?
If "yes," ask 9.

6. What have you been doing in the last 4 weeks to find work?

9. What are all of the things you have done to find work during the last 4 weeks?

Individuals can be classified as "at work" at question 1 or 2. Individuals can be classified "employed, temporarily absent" with the combination of 1 and 4, or 3 and 4. Individuals available for work can be classified as unemployed with combinations of 1 and 4, 3 and 4, 1 and 6, or 5 and 6.

Individuals are classified as employed if they say "yes" to questions 2, 3 (and work 15 hours or more in the reference week or receive profits from the business/farm), or 4. Individuals available to work are classified as unemployed if they say "yes" to 5 and either 6 or 7, or if they say "yes" to 8 and provide a job search method that could have brought them into contact with a potential employer in 9.

The Civilian Labor Force

One of the measures that comes out of the CPS is what economists call the *civilian labor force,* which consists of all civilians 16 to 65 years of age not confined to an institution. The term "civilian" is used to exclude members of the armed forces who make up a small, under 2 percent, but significant part of the labor force. Since members of the armed forces are always considered to be employed, the unemployment rate would tend to go down if we included several million people who all had jobs!

The part of the definition concerning the noninstitutional population is also intended to exclude those confined to a mental hospital or prison. After all, they can hardly be expected to be able to go out and seek, let alone hold, a job. Finally, the age limitation means that an enterprising 15-year-old working 50 hours a week cannot be counted as being either employed or unemployed--the person is simply defined as not being in the labor force.

What Does It Take To Be Employed?

Believe it or not, a person is classified as being employed if he or she worked as little as *one* hour per week for pay or profit during the survey week! A person is also considered to be employed if he or she worked 15 hours during the survey week for *no pay* in a family-owned business.[2]

Since this may not seem very rigorous, what does it take to be considered unemployed? According to Figure 4-2, a person had to have been not working during the survey week, yet be available for work and either awaiting recall from an employer or be actively seeking a job.

Have We Accounted for Everyone?

Not quite. Suppose, for example, that someone claims that they were

---

[2] Individuals are classified as employed if they answer "yes" to question 2 or 4 or if they say "yes" and work 15 hours or more in the family business or farm.

not working during the survey week--but neither were they waiting for their employer to recall them nor were they actively looking for work.[3] These people are neither employed nor unemployed. Instead, they are simply dropouts, or (officially) *discouraged workers*, and are *not* officially part of the labor force.[4] In reality, discouraged workers are fairly common. During periods of recession or in areas where the number of homeless is quite high, the number of dropouts can be significant.

How Do We Get the Unemployment Rate?

This is the easy part. After we determine the number of unemployed persons, we divide them by the size of the civilian labor force. In January 1994, the numbers looked like this:[5]

$$\text{Unemployment rate} = \frac{\text{number unemployed}}{\text{civilian labor force}} = \frac{8,696,000}{130,667,000} = 6.7\%$$

Since the monthly survey data also identify the unemployed by sex, race, age, and marital status, we could also get the unemployment rate for adult men, adult women, all teenagers, whites, blacks, black teenagers, and Hispanics. Unemployment rates for these groups are frequently reported along with the overall civilian unemployment rate.

Are Unemployment Numbers Really All That Significant?

More than you might imagine! Even a relatively small change in the monthly unemployment rate involves a large number of people. For

---

[3] The new CPS has a direct question on being available to work; availability was inferred from responses to other questions under the old CPS.

[4] Discouraged workers are now officially defined "as persons who want a job, are available to take a job, and who had looked for work within the past year but not within the prior 4 weeks because they believed their search would be futile." See Sharon R. Cohany, Anne E. Polivka, and Jennifer M. Rothgeb, "Revisions in the Current Population Survey Effective January 1994," in *Employment and Earnings*, February 1994.

[5] According to a study done by the BLS, the unemployment rate for January 1994 would have been 6.3 percent, instead of 6.7 percent, had the old CPS questionnaire been used.

example, with a civilian labor force of 130,667,000, an increase in the unemployment rate of just one-tenth of 1 percent would mean that an additional 130,667,000 individuals would be out of work. This is more than the total number of people currently living in New Haven, Connecticut, Lansing, Michigan, or Topeka, Kansas!

Finally, we might point out that the unemployment rate in the United States is generally higher than those reported in many European countries, a difference due primarily to the way the statistics are compiled. In the United States, we make an effort to *look* for the unemployed. In many other countries, people are not even counted as being unemployed until they actually show up to collect an unemployment check--which results in the unemployment rate being understated in those nations.

What About the Historical Record?

Today, most economists would agree that an unemployment rate in the vicinity of 5 to 6 percent is relatively low. Unemployment has come down significantly since 1992, but as we can see in Figure 4-3, there have been other periods when it was even lower.

One of the more interesting things is that the unemployment rate tends to vary considerably with the state of the economy. For example, whenever the economy is in a state of expansion (represented by the unshaded areas in Figure 4-2), the unemployment rate tends to fall--and somewhat slowly at that. However, when the economy is in a state of recession (represented by the shaded areas), the unemployment rate moves up rapidly. Indeed, one of the major concerns of economists is the speed at which the unemployment rate can climb. While the recent unemployment numbers in Figure 4-1 looked good, we should realize that (1) they are not especially low from a historical viewpoint and (2) they are subject to sudden change.

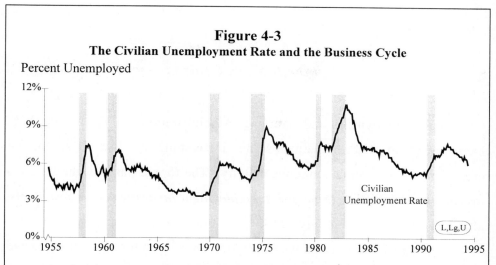

Figure 4-3
The Civilian Unemployment Rate and the Business Cycle

The unemployment rate acts like a leading indicator by turning up before a recession gets underway. Unfortunately, unemployment tends to increase fairly rapidly once a recession begins. After the recession is over, it usually takes several years for the rate to come back down to its former level.

Aside from the pain, suffering, and sheer waste of resources represented by the index, the unemployment rate has some value as an indicator of future economic activity. Although the warning period is relatively short, the series tends to be a leading indicator of future economic downturns and a lagging indicator of impending recoveries.[6]

Civilian Unemployment Rate in Brief	
Indicator status:	Leading for recessions, lagging for recoveries, unclassified overall
Compiled by:	Bureau of Labor Statistics
Frequency:	Monthly
Release date:	Normally the first Friday of the following month
Revisions:	Monthly numbers not revised, annual revisions every January for the past 5 years to account for seasonal factors
Published data:	*Economic Indicators,* Council of Economic Advisors
	Employment and Earnings, Bureau of Labor Statistics
	Su*rvey of Current Business*, U.S. Department of Commerce
	THE ECONOMIC BULLETIN BOARD, U.S. Department of Commerce
Hotline update:	(202)606-7828 for a 4- to 5-minute update on employment conditions, consumer prices, and producer prices

---

[6] The BEA inverts, or turns the series upside-down, for classification purposes (the series is not inverted in Figure 4-3). The adjustment is made for the sake of appearances only. When the series is inverted, it looks more like others that turn down before the economy turns down.

New Jobless Claims

The Employment and Training Administration (ETA) of the U.S. Department of Labor maintains an interesting cyclical indicator of employment and overall economic activity. The formal name of the series is *average weekly initial claims for unemployment insurance, state programs*, although it is more commonly called "new jobless claims."

The data are published weekly by the ETA in both seasonally adjusted and unadjusted formats. Because the weekly numbers are subject to such wide variations, a 4-week moving average is employed to smooth out the data. Figure 4-4 shows the movement of the smoothed series against the familiar recession-expansion background.

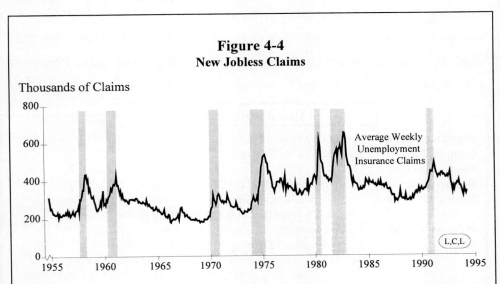

Figure 4-4
New Jobless Claims

New unemployment insurance claims are released weekly by the U.S. Department of Labor. Because the unemployment claims often vary dramatically from one week to the next, a 4-week moving average is employed to smooth the data.

Are New Jobless Claims an Economic Indicator?

Since labor is a variable cost, meaning that the number of workers employed varies with changes in the level of production, new claims for unemployment insurance are intuitively appealing as an economic indicator.

Indeed, Figure 4-4 shows that new claims tend to decline during expansionary periods and then rise several months before the recession actually begins.[7] According to the Bureau of Economic Analysis in the Department of Commerce, the series is a leading indicator when it comes to forecasting peaks in economic activity, a coincident indicator when it comes to predicting when the economy will bottom out, and a leading indicator overall. And because of the relatively uniform lead times for the turning points, the Bureau of Economic Analysis includes the series as one of the *index of 11 leading indicators* components.

Finally, a word of caution. The popular press often tends to report on individual weekly numbers rather than the moving average. Because these tend to vary so widely from one week to the next, the seasonally adjusted moving average is a much better measure of labor market conditions.[8]

New Jobless Claims in Brief	
Indicator status:	Leading for recessions, coincident for recoveries, leading overall
Compiled by:	Employment and Training Administration
Frequency:	Weekly
Release date:	Second week following close of the latest reporting week
Revisions:	Previous 2 weeks revised with each weekly release, annual revisions in January for several years back
Published data:	*Economic Indicators*, Council of Economic Advisors
	Survey of Current Business, U.S. Department of Commerce
	Unemployment Insurance Claims, weekly bulletin, Employment and Training Administration, U.S. Department of Labor
	THE ECONOMIC BULLETIN BOARD, U.S. Department of Commerce
Hotline update:	(202)219-7388 for a brief recorded message

---

[7] This series, like the unemployment rate in Figure 4-3, is inverted by the BEA.

[8] Some states tie jobless payments to earnings in a base period such as the previous quarter. This often causes people to delay unemployment filings until a more favorable base period (one with less income) can be reported.

Help-Wanted Advertising

One of the few major statistics collected by a nongovernmental agency is the index of *help-wanted advertising in newspapers*. The monthly index is compiled by The Conference Board and is available from 1951 to the present with 1967 used as the base year.

How Is the Index Compiled?

The Conference Board collects data on the number of help-wanted classified ads printed in 51 cities around the country. In each city, a count of all classified ads is taken from a single newspaper, and the total is adjusted for both seasonal patterns and the number of days in each calendar month.[9] The count for each city is then weighted according to the size of the labor market in the region and, after some other minor adjustments, compiled and released. The index is available both in a "national" format, shown in Figure 4-5, and for each of nine census regions of the country.

What About Its Value as an Indicator?

In general, the monthly help-wanted index tends to be a fairly reliable leading indicator when it comes to predicting the end of an expansion. The index tends to peak several months before the recession sets in, and the amount of lead time is fairly consistent. It tends to fall throughout the recession and then bottom out just as, or shortly after, the recession ends. Finally, the data are normally not subject to revision, which means that we do

---

[9] See *The Help-Wanted Index: Technical Description and Behavioral Trends*, Conference Board Report No. 716.

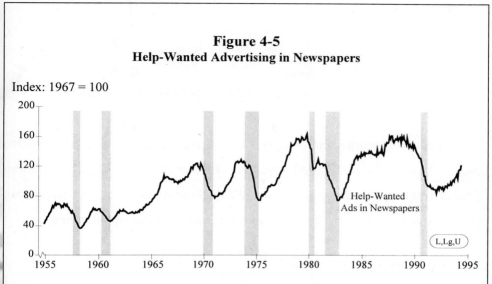

Figure 4-5
Help-Wanted Advertising in Newspapers

Index: 1967 = 100

The number of classified ads in 51 selected cities forms the basis of The Conference Board's help-wanted index. Historically, it has proved to be a fairly reliable leading indicator of impending economic downturns.

not have to wait for additional data to see how a particular month fared.

The reliability of the index is such that it is also reported by the BEA in the monthly edition of the *Survey of Current Business*. The BEA classifies the index as a leading indicator for recessions and a lagging indicator for recoveries. This means that the series has an overall rating as unclassified, but that does not diminish its value as a tool for predicting when the next recession might arrive.

Help-Wanted Advertising in Brief	
Indicator status:	Leading for recessions, lagging for recoveries, unclassified overall
Compiled by:	The Conference Board, 845 Third Avenue, New York, NY 10022
Frequency:	Monthly
Release date:	First week of following month
Revisions:	Previous month's numbers not normally revised
Published data:	Monthly Conference Board press releases
	Conference Board Report No. 716
	Survey of Current Business, U.S. Department of Commerce
	THE ECONOMIC BULLETIN BOARD, U.S. Department of Commerce
Hotline update:	None

Personal and Disposable Personal Income

Personal income sounds as if it should refer to the income people earn: their salaries, tips, and hourly wages. In a way it does, but in a more fundamental sense, *personal income* (*PI*) represents the total current income received by persons from all sources *minus* social insurance payments.

NIPA and Personal Income

GDP may be the primary measure of total output in the national income and product accounts, but it is *not* the best measure of the nation's income for two reasons. First, GDP *includes* output generated with resources owned by foreign (now called ROW for rest-of-world) residents. Since income earned by ROW residents leaves the United States, it cannot be included as part of our nation's income. Second, GDP *ignores* income earned by U.S. residents as a result of their investments abroad.

Table 4-1
Converting GDP to GNP, Billions of Current Dollars

Gross domestic product (GDP)	**$6,623.1**
Plus: Receipts of factor income from ROW	141.3
Less: Payments of factor income to ROW	145.9
Gross national product (GNP)	**6,618.6**

Final data for 1994-I (the first quarter of 1994)

Table 4-1 shows the conversion of GDP (the measure of total domestic output) to GNP (the measure of total income). The first step is to subtract the income earned by ROW residents as a result of their investments in the United States. The second is to add the income earned by U.S. residents as a result of their international investments.[10]

The rest of the NIPA components are shown in Figure 4-6. To go from GNP to a ***net national product*** (***NNP***) of $5,882.7 billion, we subtract the wear and tear on the capital stock, more formally known as ***capital consumption adjustments*** (***CCA***). The government then takes a slice of the income earned by businesses in the form of indirect business taxes,[11] and the remainder, called ***national income (NI)***, is $5,317.1 billion. This represents the sum of employee compensation, proprietors' income, rental income, corporate profits, and net interest payments in the economy.

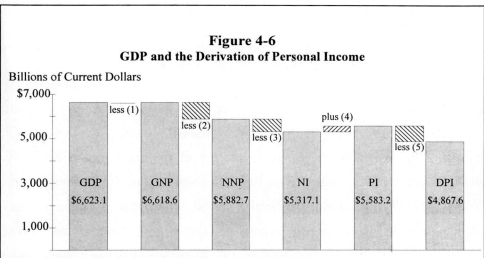

Figure 4-6
GDP and the Derivation of Personal Income

Note: data are final revised estimates for the first quarter of 1994.
(1) Factor income payments to ROW are subtracted, and factor income receipts from ROW are added to GDP to get gross national product (GNP).
(2) Consumption of fixed capital (primarily CCA) is subtracted from GNP to get net national product (NNP).
(3) Indirect business taxes are subtracted from NNP to get national income (NI).
(4) Undistributed corporate profits and social insurance payments are subtracted and transfer payments are added to NI to get personal income (PI).
(5) Tax and nontax payments are subtracted from PI to get disposable personal income (DPI).

---

[10] In the case of the U.S., the two adjustments are nearly offsetting, so that GNP and GDP are almost the same. This is not always the case for other countries. For example, Canada's, GDP is several percentage points larger than its GNP because the ROW investment in Canada was much larger than Canadian investments in the ROW.
[11] Indirect taxes are the licenses, taxes, and other fees a firm pays to do business. Several other adjustments are also made at this stage, but the category of indirect business taxes is the most important.

To get to ***personal income*** (***PI***), undistributed corporate profits (retained earnings) and contributions for social insurance payments like social security are subtracted. At the same time, transfer payments, such as unemployment compensation, welfare, and aid to families with dependent children, are added in. The result, shown in Figure 4-6, is the aggregate measure called personal income in the amount of $5,583.2 billion.

Finally, if we subtract tax and other nontax payments from PI, we get a ***disposable personal income*** (***DPI***) of $4,867.6 billion, the income people actually have left over for spending purposes.

Now That We Have It, What Can We Do with It?

Plot it, naturally, and see what it looks like.

In Figure 4-7, personal income in both current and constant dollars is plotted against the familiar backdrop of business expansions and contractions. As we can see, the trend in personal income when measured in *current* dollars seems to be up, regardless of the state of the economy. Indeed, 425 monthly statistics on PI are reported in the figure--and PI was down only 37 times during this entire period. Moreover, 9 of the monthly declines took place during recessions, while 28 took place during expansions! As a result, a monthly decline of current dollar personal income may be newsworthy, but it may not be very meaningful.

A much better measure is PI in *constant* dollars which is not distorted by inflation. This series, also plotted in Figure 4-7, shows that personal income is flat to negative during recessions and generally up during expansions. In retrospect, this is exactly the pattern we should have expected. Personal income is such a large component of GDP (84.3 percent in the first quarter of 1994) that both *should* go up and down together, even though the movements are relatively small. In fact, personal income might have been down a little more during the recessions had it not been for

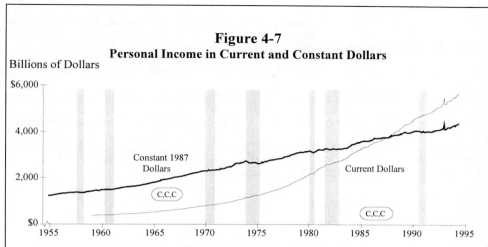

Figure 4-7
Personal Income in Current and Constant Dollars

Monthly estimates of personal income are usually reported in the press in terms of current dollars simply because current dollar estimates are available first. Unfortunately, current dollar figures almost always go up. Despite the brief delay in obtaining constant dollar figures, they are much more useful because they are not distorted by inflation.

transfer payments which acted as buffers to cushion the decline in income.[12]

On rare occasions PI can even be affected by political events. Right after the Presidential elections of 1992, many individuals who feared higher tax rates under the Clinton administration arranged to have their annual bonuses paid in December of 1992, rather than wait for January when a new tax year--and possibly higher tax rates--would apply.[13] This accounts for at least part of the $73 billion "spike" in PI that is so visible in Figure 4-7.

Because real GDP and real PI usually move together, PI in constant dollars is classified as a coincident indicator. PI in current dollars is called "an important economic measure" by the BEA but has no other status.

Are Coincident Indicators Useful?

Of course! They tell us where we are and how we are doing. They just

---

[12] According to Pauline Cypert at the BEA, reliable monthly figures for personal income in current dollars are not available prior to 1959. BEA does, however, post a constant dollar series on THE ECONOMIC BULLETIN BOARD that extends back to 1947.

[13] Under the Clinton administration, Congress made the individual income tax more progressive by adding a fourth marginal tax bracket of 39.6 percent which applies to taxable income over $250,000. The rates were also made retroactive to January 1993.

don't give us *advance* warning of where the economy is heading as do changes in leading indicators.

Finally, we should note that because personal income is one of the national income and product account components, it is on the same revision schedule as GDP that was discussed earlier on page 17. As a result, any new monthly announcement of personal income will almost always mention a revision of the previous month's figure.

Is There Anything Personal Income Doesn't Tell Us?

It tells us very little about the distribution of income. Like GDP and GNP, it is so comprehensive that we cannot tell how it is divided among those who receive it. It is entirely possible (although unlikely) that most of the increases in personal income go only to the very wealthy. Of course, the increases could go to minimum wage recipients instead, but we don't know that either.

The biggest problem is that monthly personal income and disposable personal income numbers are in *current* dollars. The reason is that the data needed to make the inflation adjustments are usually not available when the personal income figures are compiled. As a result, current dollar figures are released and reported in the press. This is unfortunate because inflation makes the series appear to grow even faster than it actually does.

Personal Income, Disposable Personal Income in Brief	
Indicator status:	Coincident for recessions and recoveries, coincident overall
Compiled by:	Bureau of Economic Analysis
Frequency:	Monthly
Release date:	End of month for the previous month
Revisions:	Preliminary and final revisions of the advance estimates
Published data:	*Economic Indicators*, Council of Economic Advisors
	Survey of Current Business, U.S. Department of Commerce
	THE ECONOMIC BULLETIN BOARD, U.S. Department of Commerce
Hotline update:	(202)606-5303 for a 3- to 5-minute message

Corporate Profits

The Bureau of Economic Analysis in the Department of Commerce compiles several series on corporate profits. The most important is ***corporate profits after tax in constant dollars***.[14] Total profits are reported for domestic financial and nonfinancial firms, with the latter including estimates for manufacturing, trade, transportation and public utilities.

The Historical Record

Two estimates of quarterly corporate profits, shown on an inflation-adjusted basis in Figure 4-7, are published. The first is a preliminary estimate

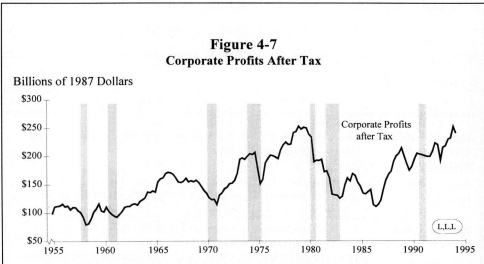

Figure 4-7
Corporate Profits After Tax

Billions of 1987 Dollars

Corporate Profits after Tax

L,L,L

The most popular of the corporate profits series is the after-tax measure shown above. Because data are collected from quarterly corporate reports, the series is only available quarterly, and then after a considerable delay.

---

[14] Other popular indicators, also leading indicators, are the *ratio, corporate domestic profits after tax to corporate domestic income* and the *corporate net case flow* series.

based on an industry sample and is released approximately 45 days after the close of the quarter. The second is a final estimate based on more complete data and is released approximately 90 days after the close of the quarter.[15]

Corporate Profits as a Leading Indicator?

We often think of the net corporate profits series as being an indicator of the general financial health of the corporate sector. Indeed, this is exactly what the series is intended to measure.

At the same time, it turns out that the series tends to be a leading indicator of future economic activity. In fact, this is the case even when the series is measured in terms of current (inflation-biased) dollars. With the single exception of the 1973-1974 recession, corporate profits have turned down well in advance of the general decline in economic activity.

Because of these patterns, the Bureau of Economic Analysis has classified the series as an overall leading indicator of future economic activity. The extent of the warning given by changes in the direction of the series may vary some, but it does give us some advance signal of future economic trends.

Corporate Profits in Brief

Indicator status:	Leading indicator for recessions and recoveries, leading overall
Compiled by:	Bureau of Economic Analysis
Frequency:	Quarterly
Release date:	Approximately 45 days following the close of the quarter
Revisions:	A second, final, revision appears 45 days after the first, or 90 days after the end of the quarter.
Published data:	*Economic Indicators,* Council of Economic Advisors
	Survey of Current Business, U.S. Department of Commerce
	THE ECONOMIC BULLETIN BOARD, U.S. Department of Commerce
Hotline update:	(202)606-5306 for a brief recorded message when GDP updates are available

---

[15] For example, the preliminary estimate for the financial sector is based on a sample of approximately 100 financial institutions. When more complete quarterly information is available from the FDIC, this new data is used for the final estimate.

Chapter 5

SPENDING, SALES, AND EXPECTATIONS

Consumer Spending

Overall spending by consumers is often considered to be an important measure of the economy's health. Consumer spending is monitored by the U.S. Department of Commerce and is reported on a monthly basis in both current and constant (inflation adjusted) dollars. As can be seen in Table 5-1, it is also the largest single component of GDP, accounting for more than two-thirds of all expenditures.

However, if you look in the Department of Commerce's index to current statistics, you won't find it listed under "consumer" or even "spending." Instead, it is called *personal consumption expenditures* and is listed in the *gross domestic product* and *personal income and its disposition* tables.

How Does Consumer Spending Behave over Time?

It turns out that the category of personal consumption expenditures is the *most* stable component of the economy.[1] Because of its stability and because the initial release from the Department of Commerce is in current (rather than constant) dollars, the series generally tends to go up, regardless of whether the economy is expanding or not.

---

[1] The reader may want to refer to Table 3-1 on page 45 to see how personal consumption expenditures vary with respect to other national income and product account (NIPA) components.

To illustrate, 425 months of personal consumption expenditures are plotted in Figure 5-1.[2] During this period, the current dollar series turned down only 49 times--with 37 of the declines occurring during expansions and 12 occurring during recessions![3]

Even when the series is adjusted for inflation by using constant 1987 dollars, the personal consumption expenditures series *still* manages to show modest gains during recessionary periods. During the most recent recession, which began in July 1990, personal consumption expenditures in real (constant) dollars turned down during only four of the nine recessionary months.

Table 5-1
Personal Consumption Expenditures, Current and Constant 1987 Dollars

	Current	Constant	% GDP
Gross domestic product	*$6,623.1*	*$5,269.5*	*100.0*
Personal consumption expenditures	*4,563.7*	*3,551.9*	*68.9*
Durable goods	578.0	523.4	8.7
Motor vehicles and parts	248.8	210.7	3.8
Furniture and household equipment	220.9	228.2	3.3
Other	108.3	84.6	1.6
Nondurable goods	1,382.5	1,111.8	20.9
Food	677.4	540.9	10.2
Clothing and shoes	243.7	205.9	3.7
Gasoline and oil	101.5	84.7	1.5
Fuel oil and coal	16.9	14.5	0.3
Other	343.0	265.8	5.2
Services	2,603.2	1,916.6	39.3
Housing	647.1	497.5	9.8
Household operation	257.2	223.3	3.9
Electricity and gas	117.4	101.7	1.8
Other household operations	139.8	121.6	2.1
Transportation	177.3	129.1	2.7
Medical care	710.2	472.6	10.7
Other	811.3	594.1	12.2
Gross private domestic investment	*970.0*	*889.3*	*14.6*
Net exports of goods and services	*-83.5*	*-105.0*	*-1.3*
Government purchases of goods and services	*1,172.9*	*933.3*	*17.7*

Source: THE ECONOMIC BULLETIN BOARD, July 1994 (final revised figures for the first quarter, 1994).

[2] Because of recent data revisions, the BEA does not have reliable monthly data prior to 1959.
[3] During this period, there were only three instances when monthly declines were back to back.

Figure 5-1
Consumer Spending and Aggregate Economic Activity

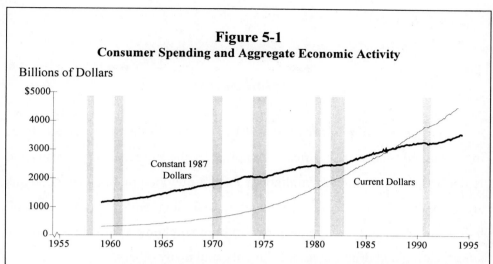

Personal consumption expenditures in current dollars, the first released by the U.S. Department of Commerce, are among the most predictable of all economic statistics. A constant dollar measure gives a better picture of spending, but it too reflects the remarkable stability of spending by the consumer sector. (Because of recent data revisions, the BEA series goes back only to 1959.)

If personal consumption expenditures are so stable, and therefore so predictable, why do we hear so much about the series in the popular media?

Perhaps the most important reason is simply that it is available. Of course, it's also so large that it is hard to ignore. The series does give us an idea of what is happening in the consumer sector, but it is really more useful for tracking long-term trends. However, it does not exhibit the type of behavior that helps us to predict changes in future economic activity.

Personal Consumption Expenditures in Brief

Indicator status:	None
Compiled by:	Bureau of Economic Analysis
Frequency:	Monthly
Release date:	End of month on the day following release of GDP
Revisions:	Revisions of previous estimates to the beginning of the previous quarter
Published data:	*Survey of Current Business*, U.S. Department of Commerce
	THE ECONOMIC BULLETIN BOARD, U.S. Department of Commerce
Hotline update:	(202)606-5303 for personal income and outlays (personal consumption)

Retail Sales

The series on ***monthly retail sales*** covers total sales for all retail stores in the United States. The series is compiled by the Bureau of the Census and is published approximately midmonth for the previous month. Breakdowns are available for a variety of industries, including building materials and hardware stores, automotive dealers, furniture and home furnishings, grocery stores, eating and drinking establishments, and many others.[4]

Collectively, sales at retail outlets make up about 40 percent of the *personal consumption expenditures* series examined earlier. The initial release of monthly retail sales data is not adjusted for inflation, although constant dollar data, shown in Figure 5-2, are available shortly thereafter.

The Historical Record

For the most part, the data reflect the *discretionary* expenditures of the consumer sector, as well as some spending at retail establishments by governmental and business units. As a result, the series tends to show a bit more movement than the personal consumption expenditures in Figure 5-1.

When retail sales are measured in terms of current dollars, the series generally tends to go up, even during recessions. When the series is adjusted for inflation, it moves more with the economy and tends to peak before the economy peaks. However, the lead time is variable, and so the series isn't very helpful in predicting a recession.

---

[4] The retail sales series is different from most NIPA data in that the monthly sales figures are not annualized. Instead, the monthly numbers report on sales for the period, and annual sales are determined by adding up the sales for each of the individual months. The series is, however, adjusted for seasonal, holiday, and trading day differences.

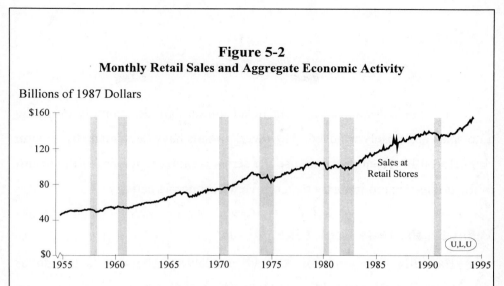

Figure 5-2
Monthly Retail Sales and Aggregate Economic Activity

Billions of 1987 Dollars

Approximately 40 percent of personal consumer expenditures takes place at retail stores. Some of the volatility of the series is due to big ticket items such as automobiles, furniture and household appliances. The series behaves as a leading indicator when it comes to predicting the end of a recession, but it is unclassified otherwise.

When the economy is in recession, and if we are trying to predict when the recession might end, the series on total retail sales is usually helpful. Since the series tends to recover before the economy recovers, the BEA has classified it as a *leading indicator* for recoveries.

Monthly Retail Sales in Brief	
Indicator status:	Leading for recoveries, unclassified otherwise
Compiled by:	Bureau of the Census
Frequency:	Monthly
Release date:	Two weeks after the close of the month
Revisions:	Advance, preliminary, final estimates released at monthly intervals
Published data:	*Economic Indicators*, Council of Economic Advisors
	Advance Monthly Retail Sales, U.S. Department of Commerce
	Survey of Current Business, U.S. Department of Commerce
	THE ECONOMIC BULLETIN BOARD, U.S. Department of Commerce
Hotline update:	None

Auto Sales

Because automobiles are big ticket durable goods, monthly domestic auto sales are closely watched. However, inroads have been made by foreign competition in recent years, and so the series is more indicative of the health of the domestic auto industry than of overall economic activity.

What Do the Data Look Like?

Basically, two kinds of data are available. The first is the dollar volume of sales as reported by the Department of Commerce. Sales are part of the GDP statistics discussed earlier and, as in the case of GDP, three releases are scheduled: an *advance* release issued on the ninth working day of the month, a *preliminary* estimate issued near the end of the month, and a *final* revised release available at the close of the second month.

The second type, and the one that receives the most attention, is in millions of units sold annually. This series is called **domestic auto sales, seasonally adjusted annual rate** and is compiled monthly by the BEA.[5] Domestic automobiles, by the way, are defined as vehicles built in Canada, the United States, or Mexico for sale in the United States.

Who Makes Domestic Automobiles?

More companies than you would imagine! At the present time, a total of 11 companies produce cars and light trucks for sale in the United States.[6] These firms, listed in Table 5-2, sold a total of 1,309,157 vehicles (763,242

---

[5] Prior to 1994, the BEA also published three monthly 10-day samples known as early, midmonth and late-month samples. This was discontinued when General Motors announced that it would no longer release 10-day sales figures.

[6] Light trucks are class 1 and 2 vehicles with a gross vehicle weight of 10,000 pounds or less.

cars and 545,915 light trucks) in May 1994.[7]

Table 5-2
Domestic Auto and Light Truck Sales in the United States, May 1994

	Domestic		Imported		Total
	Cars	Trucks	Cars	Trucks	Sales
General Motors	284,928	175,838	150	660	461,576
Ford	171,274	168,127	4,005	-	343,406
Chrysler	76,088	128,581	3,085	-	207,754
Toyota	32,447	9,970	33,297	16,042	91,756
Honda	41,037	1,922	25,327	-	68,286
Nissan	26,293	14,591	17,418	4,476	62,778
Mazda	9,006	5,187	18,161	2,421	34,775
Mitsubishi	10,224	-	6,167	2,226	18,617
Subaru	3,756	3,741	-	-	7,497
Isuzu	8	5,866	-	4,107	9,981
Suzuki	305	1,261	266	899	2,731
Totals	655,366	515,084	107,876	30,831	1,309,157

Source: *The Wall Street Journal*, June 1994.

The monthly unit auto sales are adjusted for seasonal factors and converted to an annual rate to indicate the number of automobiles that would be sold if production continued at the sample rate for a 12-month period. This information is usually available at the end of the week following the sample period.

Historical Unit Sales

Domestic auto sales on an annualized basis, shown in Figure 5-3, exhibit wide fluctuations from one month to the next. For example, unit auto sales in September 1986 were at an 11.5 million annual rate. The very next month, however, sales *fell* more than 38 percent to a 7.1 million annual rate. The fluctuations are due to things such as changing weather and interest

---

[7] A somewhat longer summary appears occasionally in *The Wall Street Journal* and lists sales of approximately 25 individual domestic and foreign manufacturers, including companies such as Saab, Audi, Alfa Romeo, Land Rover, and Daihatsu which do not produce autos in the United States. Accordingly, the data in Table 5-2 should not be used to infer any ratio of sales between domestically produced and foreign-produced autos.

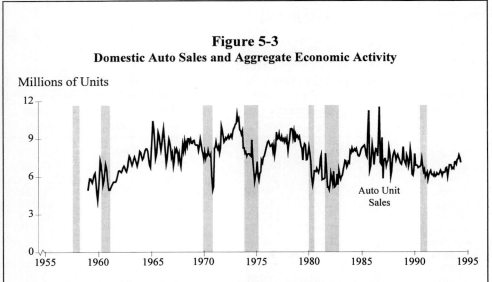

Figure 5-3
Domestic Auto Sales and Aggregate Economic Activity

Millions of Units

On a monthly basis, the domestic car sales series exhibits wide fluctuations from one month to the next. It generally turns down well in advance of an impending recession, but it has no official status as a leading indicator.

rates, as well as sales incentive programs offered by manufacturers (both foreign and domestic)--events that cannot be fully offset by seasonal adjustments to the data. Other factors, such as factory closings to retool for new models also affect the numbers.[8]

Because of wide monthly fluctuations, the industry likes to compare sales in the most recent period to sales in the same period 1 year earlier. This method of presentation is shown in Figure 5-4, where sales for 1 year are superimposed on an earlier one.

Because of the small number of domestic automotive manufacturers, it is possible to obtain unit sales directly from companies through the American Automobile Manufacturers Association or from sources like *Ward's Automotive Report*. These sources are frequently used by financial

---

[8] In November 1993, GM's Chevrolet division closed several plants to retool for newly designed Monte Carlos and Luminas. The new models were still not available in May 1994, something which contributed to a 13 percent drop in Chevrolet's car sales. Lengthy retoolings usually don't impact overall sales this much, but they can be a factor.

Figure 5-4
Domestic Auto Sales in the United States, Seasonally Adjusted Annual Rates

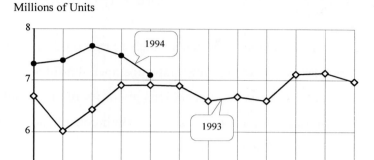

In the automobile industry, sales in any one month are usually compared to sales in the same month one year earlier. According to this figure, 1994 started out as a better year than 1993 for domestic auto sales.

publications to obtain extremely detailed breakdowns.[9]

Despite the amazing degree of detail available on automotive production, even the BEA does not publish historical data, although such data can be obtained on special request.

Domestic Auto Sales in Brief	
Indicator status:	No status with regard to future economic activity
Compiled by:	Bureau of Economic Analysis
Frequency:	Monthly
Release date:	Autos: third working day after the close of the month
	Light trucks: tenth calendar day of the month
Revisions:	Unit auto sales not normally revised, light truck sales revised back one month
Published data:	*Survey of Current Business*, U.S. Department of Commerce
	Historical data not published by the BEA, but available on request
Hotline update:	None

---

[9] The BEA derives its domestic car and light truck sales from the AAMA, and its imported sales from *Ward's Automotive Report*. Because various agencies classify recreational vehicle sales differently, auto unit sales may be reported differently by the BEA and *The Wall Street Journal*.

Consumer Confidence and Expectations

Since the consumer sector makes up such a large portion of the overall economy, it is reasonable to assume that consumer confidence about the current state of the economy, or expectations about its future, would have a bearing on current decisions to spend or save. Both considerations are often called upon to predict future economic activity.

Consumer Confidence

The most comprehensive series, the monthly *consumer confidence survey*, was initiated by The Conference Board in 1967.[10] The current survey of consumers takes place during the first 2 weeks of every month and covers 5,000 households. Data are then compiled and released during the first week of the following month.

The consumer confidence index has a base of 1985 = 100 and covers a number of categories. The major ones include appraisals of the current business situation; expectations of business conditions, employment, and income for the next 6 months; plans to buy automobiles, homes, and major appliances in the next 6 months; and questions on vacation plans. This index is available on a regional basis and is also broken down by age of household head and household income.

Overall, the series works fairly well as a leading indicator. As shown in Figure 5-5, it tends to peak before the economy peaks and to turn up before the economy turns up. It can be somewhat volatile, with monthly changes sometimes in excess of 10 percent, but it is widely watched by the business

---

[10] See the *Consumer Confidence Survey*, a monthly report from the Consumer Research Center, The Conference Board, 845 Third Ave, New York, NY 10022.

community as an indicator of future consumer spending.

Consumer Expectations

The Institute for Social Research at the University of Michigan compiles another survey of consumers called the ***index of consumer sentiment***. The index is based on a random monthly sample of 500 selected from all states except Alaska and Hawaii. The sample is closed, which

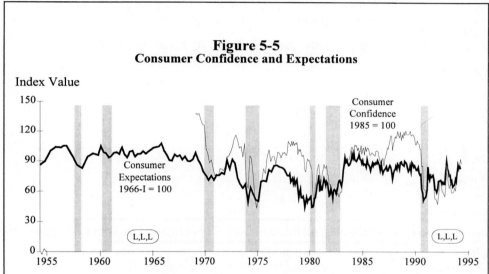

Figure 5-5
Consumer Confidence and Expectations

Consumer expectations peak a little earlier than consumer confidence, but they both function as leading economic indicators. The longer series prepared by the University of Michigan is one of the components of the *index of 11 leading indicators.*

means that only the individuals initially selected for the sample are contacted for the survey. Since the sample is random, a new group of consumers appears in the sample every month.[11]

The survey covers five major categories reported as separate indices: personal finance, current and expected; business conditions, current and expected; and buying conditions. The results of the survey are compiled and

---

[11] Although some respondents may be contacted again later on for specialized tracking purposes.

made available for release no later than the first week of the following month.[12]

One of the subcomponents of the consumer sentiment series, the ***index of consumer expectations***, performs so well as an indicator of future economic activity that it is included as one of the individual components in the composite *index of 11 leading indicators* put out by the U.S. Department of Commerce.[13] The index of consumer expectations, also shown in Figure 5-5, tends to peak somewhat earlier than The Conference Board's confidence measure and tends to recover somewhat earlier as well. Both series are widely followed, and both are used to forecast impending economic developments.

Consumer Confidence and Expectations in Brief

Indicator status:	Both series are leading for recessions, recoveries, and overall
Statistic:	*Consumer Confidence,* The Conference Board
	Index of Consumer Sentiment, Institute for Social Research, University of Michigan
Frequency:	Monthly (both)
Release date:	First week of following month (both)
Published data:	*Consumer Confidence Survey*, a monthly Conference Board report
	Survey of Current Business, for consumer sentiment data
	THE ECONOMIC BULLETIN BOARD, U.S. Department of Commerce
Hotline update:	(202)606-5361 for updates on leading index component series as they become available

---

[12] The monthly reports are available on a subscription basis. For further information contact Surveys of Consumers, 426 Thompson, 3084 ISR, University of Michigan, Ann Arbor, MI, 48106-1248.

[13] The Conference Board also compiles a consumer expectations series. This gives us four measures that are sometimes confused with one another: The Conference Board has surveys on consumer confidence *and* consumer expectations; the Institute for Social Research at Michigan reports on consumer sentiment *and* consumer expectations.

Chapter 6

PRICES, MONEY, AND INTEREST RATES

The Consumer Price Index

The consumer price index, or CPI, is one of the most comprehensive statistical measures compiled by the Bureau of Labor Statistics. In fact, the BLS actually computes two measures. The first is the *CPI for all urban consumers* (*CPI-U*), which covers about 80 percent of the total population. The second, which overlaps the first, is the *CPI for urban wage earners and clerical workers* (*CPI-W*) and covers about 32 percent of the population. Each index is a measure of the average change in prices for a fixed market basket of goods and services used by consumers.

When consumer prices are reported, the reference is to the CPI-U because of its broader coverage. It is not, however, the same as a cost-of-living index because it does not reflect the changes in buying patterns that consumers would probably make as they adjust to relative price changes.[1]

Constructing the Sample

The index is based on a hypothetical "market basket" of goods and services that consumers buy for day-to-day living. Price changes are determined by repricing the same market basket over and over again at regular (usually monthly) intervals and comparing the total cost of the most recent market basket with the cost of the sample basket in some base period.[2]

---

[1] See "Chapter 19. The Consumer Price Index," in the *BLS Handbook of Methods*, Bulletin 2414.
[2] Base periods are usually updated every 10 years. The last major revision was in 1987.

The selection of the types of items (not the brand names) consumers purchased most for the sample was based on surveys of consumers in 1982-1984. From this, the BLS constructed a market basket containing approximately 90,000 items in 364 product categories to include in the monthly analysis.

The entries in Table 6-1 illustrate the process. First, seven major product groups (PGs, such as food and beverages, housing, and transportation) were identified. Next, the product groups were divided into 69 expenditure classes (ECs). The ECs were then divided into 207 different strata, or types of items, and finally, 364 entry level items (ELIs) were selected. The latter represent the individual items in the survey whose prices will be tallied and then compared to their prices in a base period.

Table 6-1
Entry Level Items in the CPI

PG#1: Food and Beverages
    EC#1: Cereals and Cereal Products
        Strata #1: Flour and prepared flour mixes
            ELI#1: Flour
            ELI#2: Prepared flour mixes
        Strata #2: Cereal
            ELI#3: Cereal
        Strata #3: Rice, pasta, and cornmeal
            ELI#4: Rice
            ELI#5: Macaroni, similar products, and cornmeal
    EC#2: Bakery Products
PG#2: Housing
PG#3: Apparel and Upkeep
PG#4: Transportation
PG#5: Medical Care
PG#6: Entertainment
PG#7: Other Goods and Services

As you can see in the table, five items (starting with flour and ending with macaroni, similar products, and cornmeal) represent the cereals and cereal products expenditure class. Each of the remaining expenditure classes are stratified, and items are selected for each stratum until 364 entry level items are available for the sample.

Using cereal for our example, let's examine how the BLS determines where and how to price it. First, it identifies 85 geographically distributed sampling areas containing approximately 20,000 retail to be visited every month. At each outlet a BLS field survey representative selects a particular brand of cereal based on probability techniques. For example, each brand in a given store might be assigned a weight based on the relative amount of shelf space it occupies.[3] A random-number table is then used to select one of the brands for inclusion in the sample. Since this process also goes on at other outlets, different name brands are chosen so that *all* brands are very likely to appear in the total sample. Once the individual prices are collected from the outlets, the *average* price of a box of cereal is obtained.

When average prices are determined for each entry level item in the market basket, they are added up and then expressed as a percentage of their 1982-1984 total. This CPI, shown in Figure 6-1, is used to compare price levels over time. So when the CPI reached 147.5 in May 1994, it meant that the total market basket amounted to 147.5 percent of its base period cost, or that a representative item costing $1 in the base period cost $1.475 in May 1994.[4]

In all, prices are collected on 90,000 items every month. For other categories, such as housing, the BLS collects monthly prices from approximately 20,000 owner and 40,000 rental units. The amount of effort expended every month to compile the index of consumer prices is staggering!

Using the CPI

If we want to determine the rate of inflation, all we need to do is to

---

[3] We say "might" because other probability techniques are also used.
[4] This can be done for any two periods by dividing the new CPI by the old CPI. For example, the CPI was 127.4 in January 1990 and 146.2 in January 1994. Therefore, a representative item costing $1 in January 1990 cost 146.2/127.4 = 1.148, or $1.148 in January 1994.

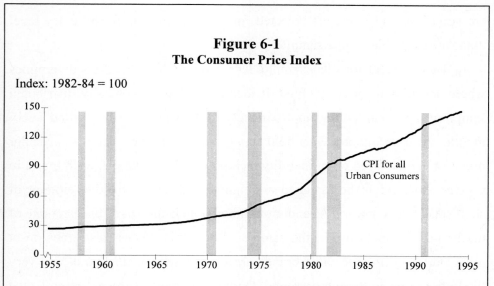

Figure 6-1
The Consumer Price Index

Index: 1982-84 = 100

The consumer price index by itself tells us very little other than how the level of prices in one period compares to another. For example, the May 1994 CPI of 147.5 in this figure tells us that prices were 47.5 percent higher than in the 1982-1984 base period.

compute the percentage change in the CPI. To illustrate, suppose that the CPI was 140.3 for 1992 and 144.6 for 1993. The annual rate of inflation would then be computed as:

$$\text{inflation rate} = \frac{144.6 - 140.3}{140.3} \times 100 = 3.06 \text{ percent}$$

When annual inflation is estimated using 1-month changes, the BLS computes the percentage change in the CPI for the most recent month, adjusts the change for seasonal variations, and then converts it to an annualized basis. However, annualized estimates based on 1-month changes often result in relatively wide swings in the inflation rate, so it is generally preferable to compute the change over longer periods such as the 6-month spans shown in Figure 6-2.

Because it is so comprehensive, the CPI is used to deflate (or convert to constant dollars) other series such as retail sales and hourly or weekly earnings. According to the Bureau of Labor Statistics, the CPI affects the

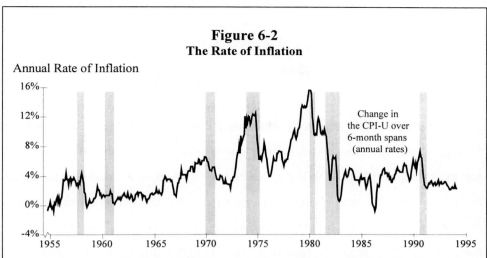

Figure 6-2
The Rate of Inflation

The annual rate of inflation is determined by annualizing the monthly changes in the CPI, although a 6-month moving average is often used to smooth some of the erratic monthly movements. Inflation appears to get worse in the latter stages of an inflation, but the series does not have any special status as an indicator of future economic activity.

income of nearly 70 million persons: over 43 million social security beneficiaries, nearly 22 million food stamp recipients, and approximately 4 million military and Federal Civil Service retirees and survivors. It is also used in escalator clauses for more than 3 million workers covered by collective bargaining agreements, and changes in the CPI affect more than 24 million children who eat lunch at school. Last but not least, the CPI has been used to adjust tax brackets for the Federal income tax code ever since they were indexed in 1985.

The Consumer Price Index in Brief

Indicator status:	None
Compiled by:	Bureau of Labor Statistics
Frequency:	Monthly
Release date:	eighth through nineteenth of the following month
Revisions:	Seasonal revisions in January for up to 5 years
Published data:	*Economic Indicators*, Council of Economic Advisors
	CPI Summary News Release, Bureau of Labor Statistics
	DEPARTMENT OF LABOR BULLETIN BOARD, U.S. Department of Labor
	THE ECONOMIC BULLETIN BOARD, U.S. Department of Commerce
Hotline update:	(202)606-6994 for consumer and producer prices, or (202)606-7828

The Producer Price Index

Another price series is the ***producer price index (PPI)***, which measures average changes in selling prices received by domestic producers for their output. Until 1978 the series was known as the ***wholesale price index***, but the title was changed to emphasize that the series measures only price changes between the producer and the *first* purchaser of the product. It does not measure price changes that occur between any other intermediaries, or even between the final wholesaler and the retailer who buys the product for resale to the public.

The Historical Record

Figure 6-3 shows the level of the PPI since 1955. The CPI (or CPI-U to be exact) is also shown for comparison purposes.[5]

Like the CPI, the PPI is broadly based. It includes price changes in approximately 500 industries and incorporates data contained in over 3,000 separate commodity price indices.

Historically, most of the interest in producer prices has focused on their eventual impact on consumer prices. If prices go up at the factory, it stands to reason that consumers will pay more later on. Figure 6-3 shows that there is a fairly close relationship between the two measures, although the PPI has fallen behind in recent years.

The difference is largely due to the coverage by each series. For one thing, the PPI measures price changes only when the product is first sold by the producer. If a number of intermediaries are involved, the percentage

---

[5] The PPI has a base of 1982 = 100 whereas the CPI-U has a base of period of 1982-84 = 100.

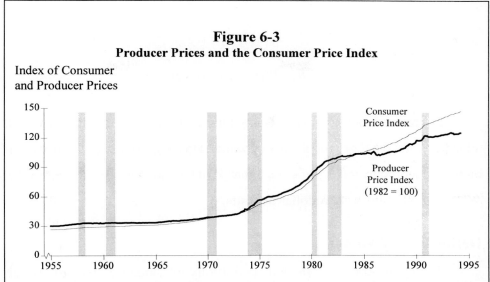

Figure 6-3
Producer Prices and the Consumer Price Index

The PPI has not kept pace with the CPI in recent years, in part because of differences in coverage between the two series. When changes in the PPI are plotted over 6-month spans, the series appears much like Figure 6-2 with prices rising sharply late in the expansion and then declining shortly thereafter.

price increase to the consumer could be higher than the initial increase at the factory. For another, the PPI covers *goods*, while *services* are largely ignored. Finally, the PPI does not cover imported items, which make up a substantial part of consumer purchases.

Increases in the PPI frequently lead to increases in the CPI. However, it is possible to have increases in the CPI without corresponding increases in the PPI because of the way services and imported goods are treated.

The Producer Price Index in Brief	
Indicator status:	None
Compiled by:	Bureau of Labor Statistics
Frequency:	Monthly
Release date:	Second week of the following month
Revisions:	Up to 4 months back
Published data:	*Economic Indicators*, Council of Economic Advisors
	DEPARTMENT OF LABOR BULLETIN BOARD, U.S. Department of Labor
	THE ECONOMIC BULLETIN BOARD, U.S. Department of Commerce
Hotline update:	(202)606-7828 for a menu-driven update of the PPI, CPI and other labor market conditions

The Money Supply

Economists define money as anything that serves as a unit of account, a medium of exchange, and a store of value. However, the exact definition of money is complicated by the fact that it takes so many different forms, ranging from coins to Eurodollar deposits.[6]

Definitions of Money

The Fed employs several definitions of money, two of which correspond to the functions of money described above.[7] One is called *M1* and is the transactional component of the money supply, or the part most closely identified with money's role as a medium of exchange. As can be seen in Table 6-2, this definition of the money supply includes coins, paper currency, traveler's checks, demand deposits, NOW accounts, credit union share drafts, and other checkable deposits.

If we want to consider money's role as a store of value as well as a medium of exchange, the definition is expanded to include other, and sometimes lesser known, forms of holding money. These include overnight repurchase agreements, overnight eurodollars, savings deposits, small denomination time deposits, and general purpose and broker/dealer money market funds. This broader-based definition of money is known as *M2*. The individual components of M1 and M2, as listed in the Fed's weekly *Statistical Release H.6*, are presented in Table 6-2.

---

[6] Eurodollar deposits are dollar-denominated deposits in banks located in foreign countries.

[7] A total of four definitions--M1, M2, M3, and L--are currently used by the Fed. M1 and M2 are the only monetary measures that are useful for predicting changes in future economic activity. See the *Federal Reserve Bulletin* for more on measures of M3 and L.

Table 6-2
Components of the Money Supply, Billions of Current Dollars

1.	Coins and paper currency	$337.3
2.	Traveler's checks	7.9
3.	Demand deposits	378.9
4.	Other checkable deposits (NOW accounts, share drafts)	409.1
	M1	**$1,133.2**
5.	Overnight repurchase agreements	$76.2
6.	Overnight Eurodollars	18.3
7.	Savings deposits	1,216.8
8.	Small denomination time deposits	767.5
9.	General purpose and broker/dealer money market funds	364.5
	M2 = (M1 plus lines 5-9)	**$3,576.6**

Source: *Statistical Release H.6*, July 7, 1994, Federal Reserve Board of Governors.

The Historical Record

Since the money supply is managed by the Federal Reserve System, we would expect that some variation in the money stock is possible over time. Money (like any other commodity) can also be measured in terms of current or real dollar amounts, the latter being preferable if we want to compensate for the distortions of inflation.

Figure 6-4 shows the levels of M1 and M2 from 1955 to the present. According to the figure, both definitions of money tend to act as leading indicators, although there is more variation in M2 than in M1 because of the monetary policy actions of the Fed. Whether intentional or not, M2 behaves in a reliable and predictable pattern, so much so that it has been classified as a leading indicator for both recessions and recoveries and is even included as one of the component series in the composite *index of 11 leading indicators*.

If we were to consider *changes* in the level of the money supply (as we did with inventories), we would find that changes in M1 also act as a leading indicator. Changes in the level of M2, however, receive an overall rating of

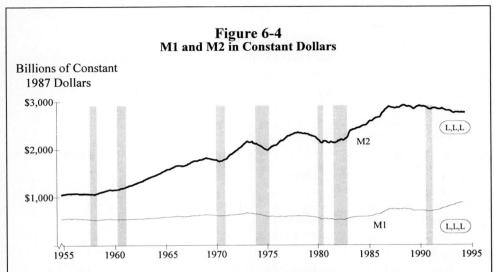

Figure 6-4
M1 and M2 in Constant Dollars

The levels of M1 and M2 have leading indicator status according to the BEA. The percentage change in the level of M1 (not shown) is also a leading indicator for recessions and recoveries. The percentage change in the level of M2 (also not shown) is a leading indicator for recessions but is unclassified otherwise.

unclassified from the BEA even though the series is a leading indicator for recessions.

Finally, some studies have found a strong, if somewhat delayed, link between changes in the level of M2 and prices. Because of this, many economists like to keep an eye on the growth of the M2 since it may indicate increased rates of inflation later on.

M1 and M2 in Brief

Indicator status:	Both series: leading for recessions, recoveries, and overall
Compiled by:	Federal Reserve Board of Governors
Frequency:	Weekly
Release date:	4:30 p.m. Thursdays for the previous week
Revisions:	None
Published data:	*Statistical Release H.6,* Federal Reserve Board of Governors
	Federal Reserve Bulletin, Federal Reserve Board of Governors
	Survey of Current Business, U.S. Department of Commerce
	THE ECONOMIC BULLETIN BOARD, U.S. Department of Commerce
Hotline update:	None

The Prime Rate

Historically, the *prime rate* was the rate banks charged their best customers. Because of this, it received wide publicity as the lowest rate available from banks. The prime rate is not quite the same as the rate actually paid, but it is still widely watched.

If You Get the Prime Rate, Do You Actually Pay It?

That depends. Suppose a business borrows $100,000 at a 10 percent prime rate. However, the company may not get the use of all of the funds because the bank may require a *compensating balance*, or a deposit (usually interest free), in the amount of $5,000. On a simple interest basis, the company is really paying $10,000 to get the use of $95,000, for a 10.53 percent simple rate.

Another bank may have an identical prime but a different compensating balance requirement in the amount of $10,000 per $100,000 borrowed. A borrower at this bank would still pay 10 percent on the $100,000 for an interest cost of $10,000 but have access to only $90,000, for an 11.11 percent simple rate.

The Historical Record

Figure 6-5 shows that the prime rate appears to adjust in steps, or stages. That is, it stays at one level for awhile and then adjusts to a new one. There are two reasons for this. First, banks are more inclined to change the compensating balance requirement than the prime, especially when interest rates are rising. Second, the official prime rate statistics compiled by the Fed represent the prevailing level rather than averages of the existing rates charged by banks.

The Fed determines the predominant prime rate by surveying the 25 major banks listed in Table 6-3. Once the predominant prime is established, the Fed waits for the majority of the banks to adopt a new rate before the prime is recomputed. Occasionally, a bank not on the list may change its rate, and the action may be widely reported in the press, but it will have no effect on the official predominant prime rate statistics compiled by the Fed.

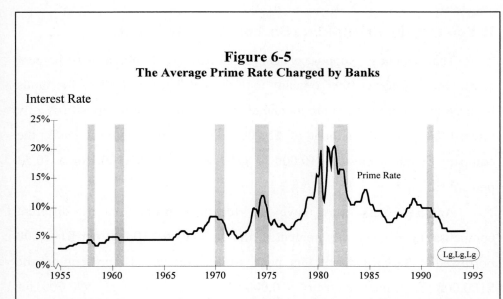

Figure 6-5
The Average Prime Rate Charged by Banks

The BEA refers to this series as the "average" prime rate charged by banks, but the series is exactly the same as the "predominant" prime compiled by the Fed. If 13 banks in the Fed sample charge a prime rate of 7 percent, and if the remaining 12 charge 9 percent, the predominant prime will be 7 percent--so it's clearly *not* the average.

Because banks can increase effective interest rates by changing the compensating balance, the prime is a lagging indicator for both recessions and recoveries. Changes in the prime rate usually make headlines, but the changes usually just reflect other interest rate changes that have already taken place.

Table 6-3
Banks Used to Determine the Predominant Prime Rate

Boston	First National Bank of Boston
New York	Bank of New York
	Bankers Trust Company
	Chase Manhattan Bank, N.A.
	Chemical Bank
	Citibank, N.A.
	First Fidelity Bank N.J., N.A.
	Marine Midland Bank, N.A.
	Morgan Guaranty Trust Company of N.Y.
	National Westminister Bank, U.S.
Philadelphia	Corestates Bank, N.A.
Cleveland	Mellon Bank, N.A.
	PNC Bank, N.A.
	Society National Bank
Richmond	Wachovia Bank of N.C., N.A.
Atlanta	First Union National Bank of Florida
Chicago	First National Bank of Chicago
	Commercial Bank - Detroit
	NBD Bank, N.A.
	Continental Bank, N.A.
Dallas	Nationsbank of Texas, N.A.
	Bank One Texas, N.A.
San Francisco	Bank of America N.T.& S.A.
	Wells Fargo Bank, N.A.
	First Interstate Bank, CA

Source: The Federal Reserve System, Division of Monetary Affairs, June 21, 1994.

The Prime Rate in Brief

Indicator status:	Lagging for recessions, recoveries, and overall
Compiled by:	Federal Reserve Board of Governors
Frequency:	Weekly
Release date:	Monday for the previous week ending Friday
Revisions:	None
Published data:	*Federal Reserve Bulletin,* Federal Reserve Board of Governors
	Statistical Release H.15, Federal Reserve Board of Governors
	Survey of Current Business, U.S. Department of Commerce
	THE ECONOMIC BULLETIN BOARD, U.S. Department of Commerce
Hotline update:	Limited information on (202)452-6459

The Discount Rate

In its role as a central bank, the Federal Reserve System is required to lend funds to other financial institutions. The **discount rate** is the interest rate the Fed charges on these borrowed funds. Unlike other interest rates, the discount rate is not a competitive rate--it is a monetary policy tool used to control the money supply. As such, the discount rate affects the general level of credit, and eventually employment, prices, and overall economic activity.

Early Development

When the Fed was first organized in 1913, the discount rate was intended to be the primary tool of monetary policy. In the 1920s, however, the Fed discovered that interest rates could also be affected by buying and selling government bonds, a function now managed by the Federal Open Market Committee (FOMC).

It may seem redundant to have an independently determined discount rate coexist with FOMC activities, but this arrangement has two advantages for the Fed. First, the discount rate is set in conjunction with the regional Fed banks, fostering an appearance of participation in the monetary policy decision-making process.[8] Second, it generates an "announcement effect" which serves as a source of policy information for Fed watchers.

---

[8] An article in *Economic Commentary* by the Federal Reserve Bank of Cleveland explains how the discount rate is set:

> The mechanics of setting the discount rate are not complicated. The Board of Directors of each of the 12 Federal Reserve Banks is required to recommend a rate setting for its Bank to the Board of Governors of the Federal Reserve System no less frequently than every two weeks. If the Board of Governors approves the recommendation, typically it will notify any of the other 12 Banks that have not made the same recommendation so that their Boards of Directors have an opportunity to act simultaneously. If the Board of Governors thinks that a change is called for when none of the 12 Banks has recommended a change, it may make informal efforts to elicit a recommendation. (July 15, 1989.)

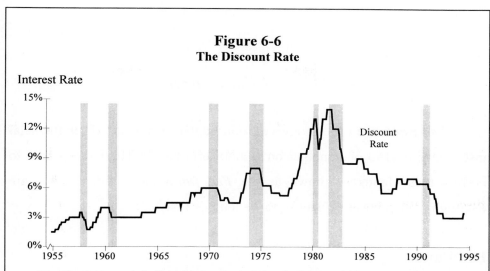

Figure 6-6
The Discount Rate

The discount rate is believed by many to be an indicator of future monetary policy. Because it is a discretionary rate intended to influence aggregate economic activity, it has no status as an indicator of future economic activity.

The Historical Record

Because the discount rate is a discretionary rate, it changes only infrequently. The rise of the discount rate at the end of each expansion, shown in Figure 6-6, reflects the Fed's concern with controlling inflation as much as anything. The discount rate has no official status as an indicator of future economic activity, even though it (as do most other interest rates) appears to lag changes in overall economic activity.

The Discount Rate in Brief

Indicator status:	None
Compiled by:	Federal Reserve Board of Governors
Frequency:	Weekly
Release date:	Monday for the previous week ending Friday
Revisions:	None
Published data:	*Federal Reserve Bulletin,* Federal Reserve Board of Governors
	Statistical Release H.15, Federal Reserve Board of Governors
Hotline update:	None

The Fed Funds Rate

Fed funds are excess reserve balances that banks and other financial institutions lend to one another on a short-term basis. The interest paid to borrow these funds is known as the *Fed funds rate*. Most loans are overnight, although some may be for as long as 3 days.

Fed Funds

Historically, member banks of the Federal Reserve System were required to keep deposits at the Fed as reserves against savings accounts and checking deposits. If a bank had excess reserves, it would often lend the surplus funds to another member bank on an overnight or weekend basis. Since the Fed did not pay interest on the reserves, member banks had little incentive to keep more funds than they needed with the Fed. Banks that borrowed the excess reserves often did so to shore up their own reserves which they also kept at the Fed.

When the loans were made, the funds never really left the Fed--hence the term "Fed" for Federal Reserve funds. All the banks needed to do to make the transaction was to notify the regional Fed bank that reserve funds were to be transferred to another bank's account for a short period of time, after which the funds would be transferred back.

Over time, Fed funds took on a more generic meaning as the practice of borrowing one another's reserves expanded to financial institutions outside the Federal Reserve System.[9] Today, financial institutions tend to deal with one another through the Fed since all depository institutions have access.

---

[9] Nonmember state banks, for example, might lend reserves to one another under this system.

A Leading Indicator

The history of the Federal funds rate since 1955 is presented in Figure 6-7. Like most other interest rates in the economy, it has an overall classification as a lagging indicator.

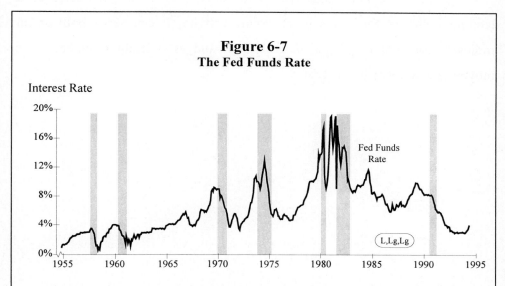

Figure 6-7
The Fed Funds Rate

Fed funds are short-term reserves that banks and other financial institutions lend to each other overnight or for a few days at a time. The Fed funds rate is the *only* interest rate that acts as a leading indicator for recessions, even though it is classified as lagging overall.

Unlike other interest rates, however, it is the *only* interest rate followed by the Bureau of Economic Analysis that is classified as a leading indicator for peaks in overall economic activity.[10] As such, it is usually the first interest rate in the economy to turn down in the face of an impending recession.

This behavior is probably due to the way in which the Federal Reserve

---

[10] The discount rate on new 91-day Treasury bills and the yield on long-term Treasury bonds are both coincident indicators for peaks in economic activity. The yields on high-grade corporate bonds and secondary market yields on FHA mortgages, as well as the average prime rate charged by banks, are all lagging indicators when it comes to predicting peaks in economic activity.

System conducts monetary policy. If the economy shows signs of entering a recession, the Fed may pump excess reserves into the banking system to keep the economy going. This practice increases the overall amount of reserves in the system and lowers the price that others pay to borrow them.

Because the Fed funds rate is the only interest rate classified as a leading indicator for peaks in economic activity, it can serve both as an indicator for future changes in real GDP and as a leading indicator for movements in other interest rates.

The Fed Funds Rate in Brief

Indicator status:	Leading for recessions, lagging otherwise
Compiled by:	Federal Reserve Board of Governors
Frequency:	Weekly
Release date:	Monday for the previous week ending Friday
Revisions:	None
Published data:	*Federal Reserve Bulletin,* Federal Reserve Board of Governors
	Statistical Release H.15, Federal Reserve Board of Governors
	Survey of Current Business, U.S. Department of Commerce
	THE ECONOMIC BULLETIN BOARD, U.S. Department of Commerce
Hotline update:	None

The Treasury Bill Rate

The **Treasury bill rate** is one of the most important short-term interest rates in the economy. Treasury bills (T-bills) are available to a wide range of investors, and they are auctioned weekly and traded daily.[11] As a result, the rate on T-bills reflects the most current market forces of supply and demand.

The Historical Record

The history of interest rate movements for Treasury bills is shown in Figure 6-8. For purposes of comparison, the prime rate is also shown.

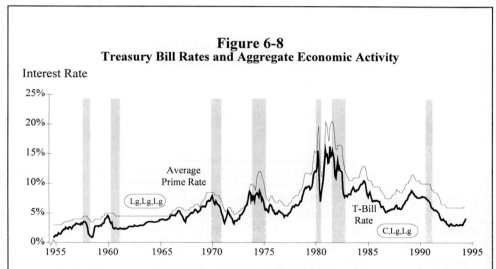

Figure 6-8
Treasury Bill Rates and Aggregate Economic Activity

The T-bill rate is one of the most competitive rates in the economy and as such is a good indicator of changes in the supply and demand for funds. In comparison, the average prime tends to adjust to the T-bill rate after a brief lag.

---

[11] A Treasury bill is a short-term obligation with a maturity of 13, 26, or 52 weeks. T-bills have minimum denominations of $10,000 and do not pay interest directly because they are sold on a discount basis. For example, an investor may purchase a 52-week bill for $9,300. The $700 difference between the amount paid and the amount received at maturity is the investor's interest. The $700 return on the $9,300 investment is a yield of $700/$9,300 = 0.0753, or 7.53 percent.

Since the T-bill rate adjusts so quickly to market forces, it changes earlier than the prime rate. The series behaves as a coincident indicator for peaks in the economy, meaning that the rate turns down when the economy turns down.

It also behaves as a lagging indicator when the economy recovers from a recession, meaning that the economy recovers before the T-bill rate recovers. The overall classification of the series, like that of *all* other interest rate series, is that of a lagging indicator.

Treasury bills are traded continuously during market hours, and so rates are available daily. Summary information is published by the Fed and most financial newspapers. Because the T-bill rate is so competitive, many adjustable-rate financial securities, including some home mortgages, are tied to them.

The Treasury Bill Rate in Brief

Indicator status:	Coincident for recessions, lagging otherwise
Compiled by:	Federal Reserve Board of Governors
Frequency:	Weekly
Release date:	Monday for the previous week ending Friday
Revisions:	None
Published data:	Most financial newspapers
	Economic Indicators, Council of Economic Advisors
	Federal Reserve Bulletin, Federal Reserve Board of Governors
	Statistical Release H.15, Federal Reserve Board of Governors
	Survey of Current Business, U.S. Department of Commerce
	THE ECONOMIC BULLETIN BOARD, U.S. Department of Commerce
Hotline update:	No direct hotline since the Fed is not authorized to give out interest rates over the phone. However, other data are available on (202)452-6459

Chapter 7

FINANCIAL MARKETS, INTERNATIONAL TRADE, AND FOREIGN EXCHANGE

The Dow Jones Industrial Average

The ***Dow Jones Industrial Average*** (***DJIA***) is one of the oldest and most quoted measures of stock market performance in the United States. It is used as a proxy for the price movements of approximately 1,650 stocks on the New York Stock Exchange (NYSE).

The DJIA includes 30 representative firms, and the size of the index depends on the market price of each firm's stock at any given time. If the prices of the stocks in the average are rising, the DJIA goes up and the market is also presumed to be going up. If the prices of the 30 stocks are falling, the DJIA goes down, indicating that other stocks in the market are also presumed to be going down. Over time, some firms are deleted and others added, but the total number of stocks is kept at 30.

Early History

In 1884 the Dow Jones Corporation began to publish the average closing price of 11 active stocks in its *Customer's Afternoon Letter*, a short publication that later evolved into *The Wall Street Journal*. By 1886 the average included 12 stocks, and by 1916 it was expanded to 20. Finally, in

Table 7-1
The 30 Stocks in the Dow Jones Industrial Average

AT&T	DuPont	Minnesota Mining & Mfg.
Allied Signal	Eastman Kodak	Morgan, J.P.
Alcoa	Exxon	Phillip Morris
American Express	General Electric	Procter & Gamble
Bethlehem Steel	General Motors	Sears
Boeing	Goodyear	Texaco
Caterpillar	IBM	Union Carbide
Chevron	International Paper	United Technologies
Coca Cola	McDonald's	Westinghouse
Disney	Merck	Woolworth

Source: *The Wall Street Journal*, July 9, 1994.

1928 it was expanded to include 30 stocks. These stocks, listed in Table 7-1, have changed occasionally over the years to keep abreast of changes in the economy. Figure 7-1 explains one of the more popular charts used to present short-term movements of the average.

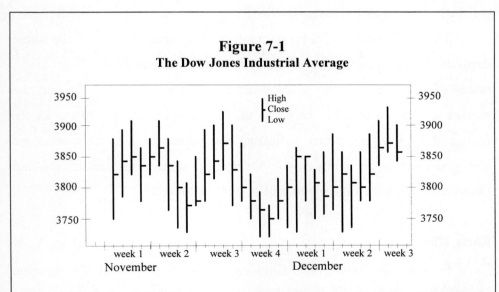

Figure 7-1
The Dow Jones Industrial Average

Each of the vertical bars shows the trading range of the DJIA during the course of a single day. The nub on the side of the bar represents the closing value for the day. Note that we cannot tell the time of day the high and low values were reached; the chart tells us only the range.

But Is It *Really* an Average?

In 1884 the index really was an average. However, stock splits soon began to cause computational problems. For example, consider a simple DJIA which, on Monday, had three stocks priced $20, $30, and $40. The DJIA for that day would be ($20 + $30 + $40)/3 = $30, or simply 30. Now, suppose that nothing happens on Tuesday except for a two-for-one split of the $20 stock (instead of holding one share of $20 stock, you now own two shares at $10, and so your wealth remains unchanged).

If we computed the DJIA on Tuesday by dividing the prices of three shares ($10, $30, and $40) by 3, the DJIA would drop to 26.7, even though investors would be no worse off than before. We could, however, compensate for the drop in the average by adjusting the *divisor*. Instead of dividing the sum of the prices by 3, we could divide by 2.667 so that the "average" would be ($10 + $30 + $40)/2.667 = 30, just as before.

Whenever a stock splits or whenever stocks on the list are replaced, the divisor can be adjusted to keep the overall average from being affected.[1] Of course, this means that the divisor must be revised frequently. By 1939, for example, the divisor was about 15; by 1950 it was below 9, and by 1981 it had reached 1.3. On July 7, 1994, the divisor was 0.3861 which means that the DJIA computation was as follows:

$$\text{DJIA} = \frac{\text{sum of 30 prices}}{\text{divisor}} = \frac{\$1,424.10}{0.3861} = 3,688.42$$

We can now definitely say that the Dow Jones Industrial Average really *is* an average . . . in a manner of speaking.

---

[1] In April 1991, the composition of the index was changed to better reflect the size of the services sector. Specifically, Navistar, Primerica, and USX were dropped from the index, while Caterpillar, Disney, and J.P. Morgan were added. The substitutions required that a *new* divisor be selected so that the DJIA on the morning when the new stocks were included would be exactly equal to the value of the index at the close of the previous day.

Are 30 Stocks Enough?

Despite the small number of stocks included in the DJIA, the companies are so large, and so many shares of stock are outstanding, that the DJIA represents about 25 percent of the total value of all stocks on the New York Stock Exchange. As a result, the movement of the DJIA coincides fairly well with that of a large number of stocks on the exchange.[2]

The companies in the DJIA do not, however, represent the smaller companies on the exchange, nor do they represent other firms listed on the American Stock Exchange or the Over-The-Counter market. The advantages of the DJIA include ease of computation--it is actually updated every 5 minutes--and the visibility given to it by the Dow Jones Corporation which publishes *The Wall Street Journal*.

Are There Other Things We Should Know?

There are probably two worth mentioning. First, any price-weighted average like the DJIA gives more weight to higher-priced stocks than it does to lower-priced ones. For example, a 10 percent increase in the price of Caterpillar (trading near $105 in July 1994) adds $10.50 to the numerator of the equation above. A 10 percent increase in the price of Westinghouse (trading near $12 at the same time) adds only $1.20 to the numerator.

The other weakness of the DJIA is that it does not adjust for stock dividends of less than 10 percent.[3] This means that it understates long-term gains in the market. Stock prices will not tend to rise as fast if some companies declare relatively small and relatively frequent stock dividends.

---

[2] For comparison purposes, a chart of the DJIA appears with the S&P 500 in Figure 7-2.

[3] Theoretically, a stock dividend (a dividend paid in stock, rather than cash) *lowers* the price of a company's stock. If a firm declares an 8 percent stock dividend, the number of shares outstanding goes up by 8 percent and the price of the stock goes down by 8 percent--leaving investors with no change in net wealth. As far as the DJIA is concerned, however, the average should go down since the price of the stock goes down.

Because the series is updated so frequently and because it has such high visibility, it is a useful measure of short-term movements of stock prices on the New York Stock Exchange. When stock price movements over longer periods are of concern, however, researchers usually turn to other series that have a broader sample and are not biased by stock dividend payouts.

Finally, the Dow Jones Industrial Average is regarded by many as an indicator of future economic activity--with the index turning down before a recession begins and then turning up before the economy turns up. Stock price movements are indeed given leading indicator status by the Bureau of Economic Analysis, but they use the Standard & Poor's 500 composite index as the "official" measure of stock prices. Even so, the reader is invited to examine Figure 7-2 to see if this leading indicator status should be extended to the DJIA.

The Dow Jones Industrial Average in Brief

Indicator status:	None formally assigned by the BEA, unofficially leading for peaks troughs, and overall
Compiled by:	Dow Jones & Co., Inc.
Frequency:	Available every 5 minutes during market hours
Revisions:	None
Published data:	Daily in *The Wall Street Journal* and in the stock market section of most newspapers
Hotline update:	(212)976-4141 for the latest market update from the Dow Jones Market Report

Standard & Poor's 500

Another popular measure of stock price performance is **Standard & Poor's 500** (**S&P 500**) composite index. Standard and Poor's Corporation published its first market index of 233 stocks in 1923. By 1957 the list had expanded to a total of 500 stocks. Today, those 500 stocks represent four major industry groupings: industrials, public utilities, transports, and finance.[4]

How Are the Firms in the Index Selected?

The selection is based on industry groupings. The market is first divided into approximately 100 subgroups ranging from aerospace to toys. Then, representative companies are selected for each industry grouping. In some cases, the firms in the subgroups are relatively small, with modest stock issues outstanding.

Moreover, unlike the DJIA, the companies in the subgroupings do not have to be listed on the NYSE; many are listed on the American Stock Exchange and the Over-The-Counter market. While the companies in the S&P 500 do not necessarily include the largest companies on the New York Stock Exchange, approximately 80 percent of the total value of the NYSE stocks are represented in the index.

How Is the Index Computed?

The S&P 500 is not a price-weighted average like the DJIA; it is a

---

[4] Until recently, the 500 stocks consisted of 400 industrial companies, 40 public utilities, 20 transportation companies, and 40 financial institutions. When a company in one category was dropped, it was replaced by another company from the same category. This practice was changed in 1988, and so the number of companies in each category varies somewhat over time.

value-weighted index reflecting the total market value of a company's stock. For each company in the sample, the total number of shares of the company's stock is multiplied by the individual price per share to get the total market value of that stock.[5] The market value for each of the remaining 499 stocks is computed in the same way, and the results are added together to get the

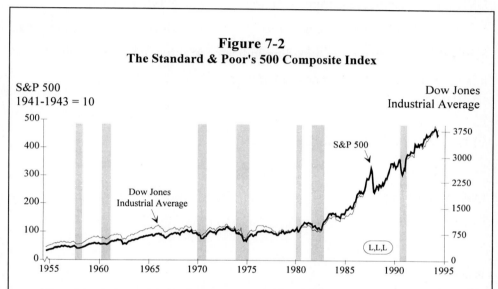

Figure 7-2
The Standard & Poor's 500 Composite Index

The S&P 500 is a value-weighted index, whereas the DJIA is a price-weighted index. Despite this difference and the difference in sample size, the two series seem to behave in a similar manner over time.

current market value of all 500 stocks in the index. The resulting total would be huge, of course, but when indexed to a base period (1941-1943 is currently used), the series becomes more manageable.

The series, shown in Figure 7-2, is slightly different from most other indices, as the base has a value of 10 rather than 100. So if the S&P 500 closes at 490, the total market value of all stocks in the index is 49 times higher (490/10) than it was in the 1941-1943 period.

---

[5] A company with 3 million shares of common stock outstanding, valued at $15 a share, would have a total market value of $(3,000,000)(\$15) = \$45,000,000$.

Is the S&P 500 Better Than the DJIA?

Different perhaps, but not necessarily better. It is more representative since 500 stocks are covered rather than 30. In addition, the value-weighted nature of the index means that it automatically adjusts for splits and stock dividends.[6] As can be seen in Figure 7-2, the S&P 500 and the DJIA are fairly close despite the difference in the sample size used by each.

In addition to its role as a proxy for stock price movements, the index generally works so well as a leading indicator of future economic activity that it is used in the BEA's composite *index of 11 leading indicators*.

Standard & Poor's 500 in Brief

Indicator status:	Leading for recessions, recoveries, and overall
Compiled by:	Standard & Poor's Corporation
Frequency:	Hourly
Release date:	Daily
Revisions:	None
Published data:	Stock report listing in most daily papers
	Economic Indicators, Council of Economic Advisors
	Survey of Current Business, U.S. Department of Commerce
	THE ECONOMIC BULLETIN BOARD, U.S. Department of Commerce
Hotline update:	(212)208-8706 for a brief taped message

---

[6] Suppose that a company listed in the S&P 500 declares a 5 percent stock dividend. The number of shares would go up by 5 percent and the price of the shares would go down by a corresponding amount, leaving the total market value of the stock--and the level of the S&P 500--unchanged. If that same company happened to be one of the 30 DJIA stocks, the index would fall slightly because the price of one of the stocks in the numerator would fall, *without* any compensating change in the divisor.

The Trade Deficit

When a country engages in international trade, it is unlikely that the value of the imports will exactly offset the value of the exports. A formal set of accounts, including the ***balance on merchandise trade*** series, tracks this international flow of goods. When services are included, the series is called the ***balance on goods and services***. Historically, this has been of less interest since the large deficits appeared in the goods category.

The word "balance" in the title allows for the possibility of a surplus as well as a deficit. However, the United States has consistently imported more merchandise than it has exported since the first quarter of 1976. Because imports have exceeded exports for so long, the word "deficit" is widely used in place of "balance." As a result, the statistic is commonly--although improperly--called the *merchandise trade deficit*.

NIPA (Again)

Trade statistics, like many other statistics generated by the U.S. Department of Commerce, are directly related to the national income and product accounts. Table 7-2 (an expanded version of Table 2-3 on page 22) follows the familiar approach of dividing the economy into sectors. This time we want to focus on the foreign sector, otherwise known as "net exports of goods and services," to see how the merchandise trade balance is computed.

The final figures for the first quarter of 1994 show the total value of all exports at an annual rate of $678.2 billion. This was offset by imports of $761.7 billion, leaving an $83.5 billion *deficit on goods and services*.

Table 7-2
The Merchandise Trade Balance, Billions of Current Dollars

	Current	Constant	% GDP
Gross domestic product	**$6,623.1**	**$5,269.5**	**100.0**
Personal consumption expenditures	**4,563.7**	**3,551.9**	**68.9**
Gross private domestic investment	**970.0**	**889.3**	**14.6**
Net exports of goods and services	**-83.5**	**-105.0**	**-1.3**
Exports	*678.2*	*615.6*	*10.2*
Merchandise (goods)	479.3	460.4	7.2
Agricultural products	43.7	36.6	0.7
Nonagricultural products	435.6	423.8	6.6
Services	198.9	155.2	3.0
Imports	*761.7*	*720.6*	*11.5*
Merchandise	624.1	614.4	9.4
Petroleum and products	41.5	56.6	0.6
Nonpetroleum products	582.6	557.8	8.8
Services	137.6	106.2	2.1
Government purchases of goods and services	**1,172.9**	**933.3**	**17.7**

Source: THE ECONOMIC BULLETIN BOARD, July 1994. Data are for 1994-I (first quarter of 1994).

The export and import categories are further divided into merchandise (i.e., goods) and services so that we can focus on the merchandise component of trade. The table shows merchandise exports of $479.3 billion and imports of $624.1 billion--leaving a $144.8 billion *deficit on merchandise trade.*

All of the trade numbers in Table 7-2 are annualized numbers, just like GDP. In other words, if things continue for the rest of the year as they did in this particular quarter, the balance on goods and services will show a deficit of $83.5 billion. Likewise, the balance on merchandise trade will show a deficit of $144.8 billion. These numbers could change in the next quarter, of course, and the annual trade balance after all four quarters are complete is again likely to be slightly different.

But What About Monthly Numbers?

In practice, data for merchandise exports and imports are collected continuously by the Bureau of the Census from declarations filed with the

U.S. Customs Office by international shippers. The trade figures are then released on both a monthly and a quarterly basis, although there is a 45-day delay after the month ends because of the nature of the data.

These initial trade figures are usually reported in terms of current, constant, and seasonally adjusted amounts. This means that the size of the deficit will be small if the report is for the month, approximately 3 times larger if the report is for the quarter, and approximately 12 times larger than the first figure if the report is for the year.

To illustrate, monthly merchandise trade balances were $-7.16, $-4.5 and $-4.05 billion, respectively, for January, February, and March of 1991. Revised figures for the quarter put the total for the three months at $-18.4 billion. The annualized deficit, based on first quarter results and adjusted for seasonal factors, was $-62.9 billion, which turned out to be fairly close to the $-73.3 billion actually recorded for the year. So, whenever trade statistics are released, we obviously need to know the coverage involved, lest we mistake a particularly large month for an unusually small quarter.

In Figure 7-3, quarterly data are used to show the balance on merchandise trade from 1954 to the present. The balance can either be shown as the difference between exports and imports or it can be plotted separately as at the bottom of the figure.

The trade balance is dependent on (1) our demand for foreign-made products and (2) our ability to sell domestically produced goods abroad. Both exports and imports have been affected by recessions, but the difference between the two--the balance on merchandise trade--is much less affected. The overall balance is important because it affects employment in the export and import industries as well as the value of the U.S. dollar.[7] Because dollars

---

[7] The relationship between the value of the dollar and the merchandise trade deficit is fairly straightforward. A strong dollar, as was the case in the mid-1980s (see Figure 7-4), usually causes imports to rise faster than exports which causes the merchandise trade balance to fall (see Figure 7-3). Eventually, the additional dollars abroad cause the value of the dollar to fall, which reverses the trend in exports and imports and improves the trade balance.

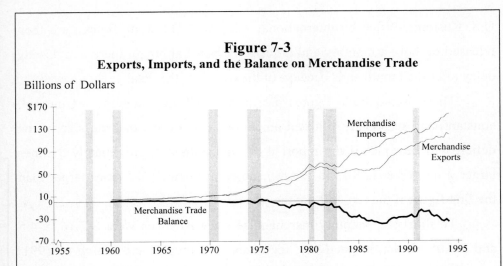

Figure 7-3
Exports, Imports, and the Balance on Merchandise Trade

Billions of Dollars

The United States has had a persistent merchandise trade deficit since the first quarter of 1976. The balance on merchandise trade, shown at the bottom of the figure, is the difference between the merchandise imports and merchandise exports at the top of the figure.

are paid to foreigners to make up for the deficit, larger deficits mean that more dollars go abroad, and more dollars circulating relative to other currencies make the dollar worth less.[8]

Merchandise Trade in Brief	
Indicator status:	None
Compiled by:	Bureau of the Census
Frequency:	Monthly, quarterly
Release date:	45 days after close of reporting month
Revisions:	One month back for seasonally adjusted data, 6 months back for constant dollar series, annual revisions in June
Published data:	*Report FT900*, Bureau of the Census
	Survey of Current Business, U.S. Department of Commerce
	THE ECONOMIC BULLETIN BOARD, U.S. Department of Commerce
Hotline update:	(301)763-5140 for merchandise trade balances, and (202)606-5362 for the more recently released of the following: merchandise trade or summary of international transactions

[8] Trade figures can be broken down by individual countries, and so it is not unusual to see a balance on merchandise trade report for a single country rather than for all countries together.

Foreign Exchange

When we talk about the value of the dollar in the context of international trade or finance, we are usually referring to the number of other currency units that can be purchased with one U.S. dollar. The amount of foreign currency that can be purchased with the dollar is called the *exchange rate*, and there are well over 200 exchange rates in the world today.

Currency Units per Dollar and Dollar Equivalents

One popular way to express an exchange rate is in *American terms*, or the cost of a single foreign currency unit in terms of U.S. dollars. For example, if one German mark can be purchased with $0.6361 American dollars (63.61 cents), then the U.S. dollar equivalent is 0.6361. Likewise, if the cost of a single yen is $0.010127, the U.S. dollar equivalent is 0.010127. Foreign exchange rates in American terms are usually the first type of exchange rates published in tables such as Table 7-3.

Table 7-3
Foreign Exchange Rates

	U.S. $ Equivalents (American terms)	Foreign Currency Units per U.S. $ (European terms)
Britain (pound)	1.5385	0.6500
Germany (mark)	0.6361	1.5721
India (rupee)	0.03212	31.13
Japan (yen)	0.010127	98.75
South Korea (won)	0.0012402	806.32

Source: *The Wall Street Journal*, July 8, 1994.

The second way to express an exchange rate is in *European terms*, or in the number of foreign currency units that can be obtained with one U.S.

dollar. For example, if one German mark cost $0.6361, then one American dollar would purchase 1.5721 German marks (1.5721 is the reciprocal of 0.6361, which is the easy way to make the computation). Likewise, one U.S. dollar would purchase 98.75 yen (the reciprocal of 0.010127).

Currency Cross Rates

If we want to observe the exchange rate between two currencies, we could express everything in terms of cross rates as in Table 7-4. This is especially helpful when neither of the currencies being traded is the U.S. dollar.

Table 7-4
Currency Cross Rates

	U.S. $	Won	Yen	Rupee	Mark	Pound
Britain	0.6500	0.0008	0.0066	0.0209	0.4135	--.--
Germany	1.5721	0.0019	0.0159	0.0505	--.--	2.4185
India	31.13	0.0386	0.3152	--.--	19.8028	47.8923
Japan	98.75	0.1225	--.--	3.1722	62.8181	151.92
S. Korea	806.32	--.--	8.1651	25.9011	512.9135	1,240.5
U.S.	--.--	0.0012402	0.010127	0.03212	0.6361	1.5385

Source: Computed from Table 7-3.

In the table, the value of each currency unit is expressed in terms of other currencies. For example, if one U.S. dollar buys 0.6500 British pounds, and if one U.S. dollar buys 1.5721 German marks, then one German mark is worth 0.6500/1.5721 = 0.4135 British pounds. Likewise, one British pound is worth 2.4185 German marks (the reciprocal of 0.4135).

Foreign Exchange Rates in Brief

Indicator status:	None
Compiled by:	Federal Reserve Board of Governors
Frequency:	*H.10* weekly, *G.5* monthly
Release date:	*H.10* Monday for the previous week ending Friday, *G.5* last day of month for the reporting month
Revisions:	None
Published data:	*The Wall Street Journal* for previous the day
	Statistical Release H.10, for daily noon buying rates in NYC
	Statistical Release G.5, for monthly noon buying rates in NYC
Hotline update:	None

The Value of the Dollar

When we talk about the value of the dollar, we are referring to its purchasing power in terms of other currencies. However, we can't evaluate the strength of the dollar by following just one or two exchange rates. The *exchange value of the U.S. dollar*--an index compiled by the Federal Reserve System to track the value of the U.S. dollar relative to a bundle of foreign currencies--remedies this difficulty. Since it is compared to an index of multiple currencies, it is our best overall measure of the dollar's strength.

How Is the Weighted Average Computed?

To compile the index, the Fed selected a group of 10 major industrialized countries substantially involved in world trade.[9] The weight of each country's currency in the index is based on the amount of global trade each one had relative to the other countries in the sample right after flexible exchange rates were adopted in late 1971. After the relative weights were determined, the series was given a base of 100 for March 1973.

Because the series is in the form of an index, individual index values have no meaning other than in relation to the base or to other index numbers. When the index goes up, the dollar is getting stronger; when it goes down, the dollar is getting weaker relative to the other 10 currencies.

The Historical Record

The index, plotted in Figure 7-4, hit a low of 84.65 in July 1980, a high of 158.43 in February 1985, and a low of 80.97 in August 1992. Changes of

---

[9] Germany, Japan, France, United Kingdom, Canada, Italy, Netherlands, Belgium, Sweden, and Switzerland.

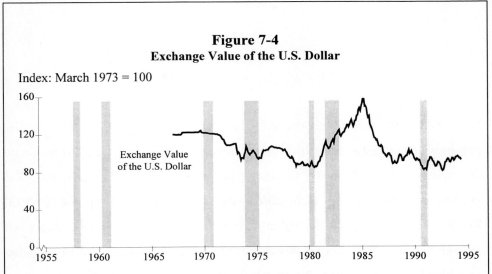

Figure 7-4
Exchange Value of the U.S. Dollar

Index: March 1973 = 100

The exchange value of the U.S. dollar, a series that extends back to 1967, is our most comprehensive measure of the international strength of the dollar. A strong dollar tends to encourage imports and discourage exports--thereby making the balance of trade worse. A weaker dollar has the opposite effects.

this magnitude have an enormous impact on the nation's exports and imports. When the purchasing power of the dollar is high, imports are relatively inexpensive and our exports relatively costly to foreign buyers--which often results in a worsening balance of trade. When the value of the dollar falls, the situation tends to reverse itself--resulting in an improving balance of trade.

Exchange Value of the U.S. Dollar in Brief

Indicator status:	None
Compiled by:	Federal Reserve Board of Governors
Frequency:	*H.10* weekly, *G.5* monthly
Release date:	*H.10* Monday for the previous week ending Friday, *G.5* last day of month for the reporting month
Revisions:	None
Published data:	*Federal Reserve Bulletin,* Federal Reserve Board of Governors *Statistical Release G.5,* for monthly rates *Statistical Release H.10,* for daily rates THE ECONOMIC BULLETIN BOARD, U.S. Department of Commerce
Hotline update:	None

Appendix

THE ECONOMIC BULLETIN BOARD

Throughout the course of this book we have made an effort to explain the importance, derivation, and application of the economic statistics we encounter in our daily lives. In addition, we have made an effort to keep the reader informed as to the sources of the data: government publications such as the *Survey of Current Business*, monthly bulletins published by the Fed, and numerous hotlines that can be accessed to provide timely updates of certain series.

One of the most important sources, and the subject of this appendix, is THE ECONOMIC BULLETIN BOARD (EBB), which can be accessed by virtually anyone with a personal computer and a modem.[1] The EBB provides a wealth of information, including the following:

- Department of Commerce press releases
- announcements of release dates for BEA statistical series
- historical files on virtually all of the BEA series, including all of the series used to create the figures in this book
- new releases of the leading and other economic indicators
- and much, much more

The remainder of this appendix is designed as a guide for those who have access to a personal computer with a modem. The discussion may seem a bit technical at times, but have patience as these obstacles are quickly overcome.

---

[1] THE ECONOMIC BULLETIN BOARD is a registered trademark of the U.S. Department of Commerce.

Logging On

The EBB is a simple menu-driven system that requires little or no expertise. You do not have to be a subscriber to take a preliminary tour of the board. Simply enter GUEST when prompted for a user ID, and you can explore (although you will not be able to download files) for approximately 20 minutes at no charge. The opening screen appears Figure 8-1.

```
                          Figure 8-1
        THE ECONOMIC BULLETIN BOARD--Introductory Screen

                  THE ECONOMIC BULLETIN BOARD (R)
                             of the
                  UNITED STATES DEPARTMENT OF COMMERCE
                     RONALD H. BROWN, Secretary

              Operated by        | Data lines:300/1200/2400 202-482-3870
    the Office of Business Analysis |          2400/9600 bps 202-482-2584
                                  |              9600 bps     202-482-2167
    Director (acting):   Ken Rogers | Telnet access:      ebb.stat-usa.gov
    EBB Manager:     Forrest Williams |
    System Operator:  Bruce Guthrie | Orders and info:        202-482-1986

     The Economic Bulletin Board is a registered Trademark of the Dept. of
    Commerce
                  Subscribers:  use your account number as your User ID
                  Nonsubscribers:      please use GUEST as your User ID

    User ID? GUEST

    TBBS Welcomes GUEST
    Your last time on was 07/05/94 10:00
    You are authorized 20 mins this call

    Type P to Pause, S to Stop listing

    ECONOMIC BULLETIN BOARD  Local time in Washington DC: 16:48 on 07/08/94
    ======== ======== =====      Connect time for this call: 00:00:16
          MAIN MENU              Port: 6    Speed: 2400
          ==== ====
    <B>ulletins       View or list system bulletins
    <F>iles           Download or search for files on system
    <T>rade Promotion Export promotion files and resources
    <P>residential    Presidential Announcements (including US Budget)
    <N>ews            New files and updates expected this week, news
                         flashes
    <U>tilities       Set default download protocol, change keyword, etc
    <C>omments        Send comments to EBB staff or read response from same

          ==><G>oodbye    <?>Help!!
```

A listing of the file areas (which changes from time to time) appears in Figure 8-2.

```
                         Figure 8-2
        THE ECONOMIC BULLETIN BOARD--File Areas

Area                   General Contents
File area #  1 ... Summaries of current economic conditions
File area #  2 ... National Income and Product Accounts
File area #  3 ... General Economic Indicators
File area #  4 ... Employment Statistics
File area #  5 ... Price and Productivity Statistics
File area #  6 ... Foreign Trade
File area #  7 ... Industry Statistics
File area #  8 ... Monetary Statistics
File area #  9 ... (Empty area)
File area # 10 ... U.S. Treasury Auction Results
File area # 11 ... Regional Economic Statistics
File area # 12 ... Energy statistics (incl COGIS files)
File area # 13 ... Trade Opportunities Reports (use "T" option)
File area # 14 ... Current Business Statistics
File area # 15 ... Press releases from the U.S.T.R.
File area # 16 ... IMI Reports (use "I" option)
File area # 17 ... Foreign Assets Control program
File area # 18 ... E. European & Former Soviet Union Trade Leads
File area # 19 ... USDA Agricultural Leads
File area # 20 ... Defense Conversion Subcommittee (DCS) Info
File area # 21 ... Miscellaneous economic files
File area # 22 ... Best Market Reports files
File area # 23 ... Software International articles
File area # 24 ... Miscellaneous trade files
File area # 25 ... Miscellaneous files
File area # 26 ... EOP: Budget of the US Govt, Fiscal Year 1995
File area # 27 ... EOP: GATT Uruguay Round Trade Negotiations
File area # 28 ... EOP: National Information Infrastructure
File area # 29 ... EOP: North American Free Trade Agreement
File area # 30 ... EOP: Health Security Plan
File area # 31 ... EOP: National Export Strategy
File area # 32 ... EOP: National Performance Review
File area # 33 ... EOP: Pres Clinton's Economic Plan (1993)
File area # 34 ... General information files
```

The Data Files

There are several types of data files on the EBB. The majority are ASCII files and can be loaded directly into a word processor or imported into a spreadsheet. Some files are already in a Lotus format and can be loaded directly into a spreadsheet (these are labeled with a .WK1 extension). Other files are in a .EXE format and will unpack into several files when run. An abbreviated listing of files in file area 8 appears in Figure 8-3.

Figure 8-3
THE ECONOMIC BULLETIN BOARD--File Area Menu

```
File area #  8 ... Monetary Statistics
           T H E   E C O N O M I C   B U L L E T I N   B O A R D
NOTE:
 Weekly and monthly historical Federal Reserve Board Bank Credit (H.8)
 data from 1988 to the present are now available as BCDETAIL.EXE.

File name         Length   Date         Contents
                  (bytes)

== Federal Reserve Board (FRB) data =================================

BC.FRB             77440   7/08/94   FRB Bank Credit           (H.8)
BCDETAIL.EXE      373174   7/08/94   Historical Weekly and Monthly FRB Bank
                                     Credit (H.8) Data from 1988 to Present
                                     (compressed self extracting file)
CNCR.FRB           10496   6/07/94   FRB Consumer Credit Report  (G.19)
EXCHANGE.FRB       17152   7/01/94   FRB Foreign Exchange Rates (G.5 & H.10)
FXRATESM.FRB        4096   7/01/94   FRB Monthly Foreign Exchange Rates G.5)
INTEREST.FRB        9095   7/05/94   FRB Selected Interest Rates (H.15)
MONEY.FRB          57600   7/07/94   FRB Money Stock Data        (H.6)
H6HIST.FRB         88960   7/07/94   FRB Historical Money Stock Data   (H.6)
RESRV.FRB          15488   7/07/94   FRB Aggregate Reserves      (H.3)
Z7.FRB             62720   6/14/94   FRB Flow of Funds           (Z.7)
VBGROUND.FRB        5248   3/01/90   Information on VRATES file from NY FED
VRATES.FRB          1920   7/05/94   Implied Volatility Rates for Foreign
                                     Exchange Options
FRB$INDX.ATL        3968   7/08/94   FRB/Atlanta Monthly US$ Index

Daily foreign exchange rate summaries, posted by the Federal Reserve
  Bank of New York:
TENFX.FRB           1664   7/08/94   10:00am EST Foreign exchange rates
NOONFX.FRB          3712   7/08/94   Noon EST Foreign exchange rates
```

Fees and Billing

The EBB has a modest registration fee which includes some connect time. After the fee is paid, the Department of Commerce will provide a user ID and a password that allows full access to all of the file areas. Time spent on the system will be recorded automatically and billed quarterly.

Index